D1030562

SOCIAL CLASS
AND
EDUCATIONAL OPPORTUNITY

Social Class

and

Educational Opportunity

by

J. E. FLOUD
(Editor)

A. H. HALSEY
F. M. MARTIN

GREENWOOD PRESS, PUBLISHERS
WESTPORT, CONNECTICUT

Library of Congress Cataloging in Publication Data

Floud, Jean E
   Social class and educational opportunity.

   Reprint of the 1957 ed. published by Heinemann,
London.
   Includes bibliographical references.
   1. Discrimination in education--Great Britain.
2. Students' socio-economic status--Great Britain.
3. Social classes--Great Britain. I. Halsey, A. H.,
joint author. II. Martin, F. M., joint author.
III. Title.
LA631.F6 1973   370.19'34   73-7195
ISBN 0-8371-6918-6

First published in 1957 by William Heinemann Ltd, London

Reprinted with the permission of Heinemann Educational Books Ltd.

Reprinted by Greenwood Press,
a division of Williamhouse-Regency Inc.

First Greenwood Reprinting 1973
Second Greenwood Reprinting 1976

Library of Congress Catalog Card Number 73-7195

ISBN 0-8371-6918-6

Printed in the United States of America

CONTENTS

Page

ACKNOWLEDGMENTS   vii

LIST OF DIAGRAMS   viii

LIST OF TABLES   ix

INTRODUCTION   xiii

PART I. SOCIAL STRUCTURE AND SECONDARY EDUCATION   1

Chapter 1. *Social Structure and Educational Policy in Contrasting Areas*   3
The Social Structure of South West Hertfordshire and Middlesbrough, Yorks   3
The Provision of Secondary Education   8

Chapter 2. *The Social Origins of Boys in Grammar Schools before and after 1944*   17
Sources of Information   17
'The Educational Ladder'   19
'Secondary Education for All'   26

PART II. OPPORTUNITY, ABILITY AND SOCIAL CLASS   31

Chapter 3. *The Social Distribution of Awards of Free and Special Places in Grammar Schools*   35

Chapter 4. *Social Class and Chances of Admission to Grammar Schools*   42
'Class Chances'   42
'Class Chances' and Measured Intelligence   44
Social Class and Competition for Free and Special Places   48
Social Class and Entry to Grammar School   50
Note on the Procedure of Selection for Secondary Schools, South West Hertfordshire and Middlesbrough   53

Page

PART III. ENVIRONMENT AND OPPORTUNITY   63

Chapter 5. *Family and Primary School Environment*
of Entrants to Secondary Schools   68
Sources of Information   68
Material Conditions at Home   71
Material Conditions at School   73
The Association of Conditions at Home
and at School   74
Attitudes and Preferences of Parents   75

Chapter 6. *Social Factors in Selection for Grammar*
Schools   87
Home Environment of Successful and
Unsuccessful Children   87
Favourable and Unfavourable Working-
class Homes   91
The Influence of School Buildings   95

PART IV. ACHIEVEMENT IN SCHOOL AND
SOCIAL CLASS   111

Chapter 7. *Length of School Life, Public Examina-*
tions and full-time Further Education   115
Length of School Life   115
Public Examinations and Entry to a
University   120
Ability and Achievement in Grammar
Schools   123

NOTE ON THE CHILDREN OF ROMAN CATHOLIC
FAMILIES IN MIDDLESBROUGH   134

CONCLUSIONS   139

NOTE ON THE CLASSIFICATION OF OCCUPATIONS   150

NOTE ON THE STATISTICAL RELIABILITY OF
TABLES   151

INDEX OF AUTHORS   152

ACKNOWLEDGMENTS

THE investigations reported here were carried out under the auspices of the Department of Sociological and Demographic Research of the London School of Economics. In 1952, when the first of the enquiries was undertaken in South West Hertfordshire, all members of the team were at the London School of Economics and we are glad to acknowledge our debt to Professor D. V. Glass for his stimulus, support and sympathetic interest in our work. Dr F. M. Martin investigated the family environment of entrants to secondary schools and analysed their performance in the selection examination. Dr A. H. Halsey undertook the work on the history and social composition of the grammar schools, and made a survey of primary school buildings and amenities. The parallel enquiries in Middlesbrough were carried out by Miss C. B. Tancock, Senior Research Assistant, London School of Economics, who also gave valuable assistance with the preparation of the statistical material in respect of both areas. Dr A. H. Halsey has been responsible with me for the preparation of the report as a whole.

We made considerable demands on the hospitality of the two areas. Our thanks are due to the Chief Education Officers of Hertfordshire and Middlesbrough for the facilities allowed us, and to the Divisional Education Officer of South West Hertfordshire and the Heads of schools in both areas. Records of the children in our samples are still being maintained and we are most grateful to those responsible for their readiness to help in what is often a laborious task.

JEAN FLOUD

LIST OF DIAGRAMS

Page

FIGURE 1 Provision of Grammar School Places for Boys, South West Hertfordshire (1904-44) and Middlesbrough (1905-44)   11

FIGURE 2 Provision of Free and Special Places for Boys in Grammar Schools, South West Hertfordshire (1904-44) and Middlesbrough (1905-44)   12

FIGURE 3 Social Origins of Boys Entering Grammar Schools, South West Hertfordshire (1884-1953)   21

FIGURE 4 Social Origins of Boys Entering Grammar Schools, Middlesbrough (1905-53)   25

FIGURE 5 Social Distribution of Free and Special Places, South West Hertfordshire (1884-1953) and Middlesbrough (1905-53)   37

FIGURE 6 Social Distribution of Measured Intelligence among Boys Entering Secondary Schools in South West Hertfordshire in 1952   45

LIST OF TABLES

Table   *Page*

1 Social Origins of Boys Entering Grammar
  Schools. South West Hertfordshire, 1884-1953   29

2 Social Origins of Boys Entering Grammar
  Schools. Middlesbrough, 1905-53   30

3 Social Origins of Boys Attending Grammar
  Schools. South West Hertfordshire (1952) and
  Middlesbrough (1953)   28

4 Social Origins of Boys Entering Grammar
  Schools with Free and Special Places. South
  West Hertfordshire, 1884-1953   40

5 Social Origins of Boys Entering Grammar
  Schools with Free and Special Places. Middlesbrough, 1905-53   41

6 Social Distribution of Measured Intelligence
  among Entrants to Secondary Schools. South
  West Hertfordshire (1952) and Middlesbrough
  (1953)   59

7 Expected and Actual Social Distribution of *Free
  and Special* Places for Boys in Grammar Schools
  at various periods. South West Hertfordshire
  and Middlesbrough   60

8 Expected and Actual Social Distribution of
  Places for Boys in Grammar Schools at various
  periods. South West Hertfordshire and Middlesbrough   61

9 Social Class and Preference for Grammar School   82

10 'Frustrated Parents'   83

11 Parents' Preferences. School Leaving Age in
   relation to choice of Secondary School   84

ix

x

Table   *Page*

12 School Leaving Age Preferred by Parents of
    Children Awarded Grammar School Places   85

13 Parents' Preferences. Further Education in Rela-
    tion to Choice of Secondary School   86

14 Social Distribution of Awards of Grammar
    School Places   100

15 Education of Parents of Successful and Un-
    successful Candidates for Grammar School
    Places   101

16 Attitudes and Preferences of Parents of Success-
    ful and Unsuccessful Candidates for Grammar
    School Places   102

17 Material Prosperity of Homes of Successful and
    Unsuccessful Candidates for Grammar School
    Places   103

18 Awards of Grammar School Places in Relation
    to the Material Prosperity of Children's Homes 104

19 Awards of Grammar School Places in Relation
    to the Education of Children's Parents   105

20 Awards of Grammar School Places in Relation
    to the Attitudes of Children's Parents to their
    Education   106

21 Awards of Grammar School Places in Relation
    to Family Size   107

22 Home Environment of Working-Class Children   107

23 Awards of Grammar School Places to Working-
    Class Children from different types of Home   108

24 Awards of Grammar School Places to Working-
    Class Children in different types of Primary
    School   108

25 Home Environment of Working-Class Children
    attending different types of Primary School   109

Table   *Page*

26 Success of Different Types of Primary School
    with Working-Class Children of varying Home
    Background   110

27 Proportion of Pupils leaving Secondary (Gram-
    mar) Schools under the age of 16 years. England
    and Wales, 1910-53   128

28 Proportion of Pupils leaving Secondary (Gram-
    mar) Schools at 17 or over. England and Wales,
    1910-53   129

29 Proportion of Pupils leaving Secondary (Gram-
    mar) Schools at the age of 16. England and
    Wales, 1910-53   130

30 Boys leaving Grammar Schools, aged under 16,
    and 17 and over, in selected periods up to 1939.
    South West Hertfordshire and Middlesbrough   131

31 Boys leaving Grammar Schools, aged under 16,
    and 17 and over, before and after the Second
    World War. South West Hertfordshire and
    Middlesbrough   132

32 Boys leaving Grammar Schools with Certificates
    and Proceeding to Further Education, before
    and after the Second World War. South West
    Hertfordshire and Middlesbrough   133

33 Social Origins of Catholic and Other Children
    Entering Secondary Schools in Middlesbrough,
    1953   134

34 Awards of Grammar School Places in Relation
    to Family Size. Catholic and Other Children.
    Middlesbrough, 1953   137

35 Home Environment of Catholic and Other
    Working-Class Children. Middlesbrough, 1953   137

Table		*Page*
36	Awards of Grammar School Places in Relation to Home Background. Catholic and Other Working-Class Children, Middlesbrough, 1953	138

INTRODUCTION

I

THIS book is the first fruits of two prolonged enquiries into the relationship between social class and educational opportunity. These enquiries arose out of a national investigation, undertaken by the London School of Economics in 1949, into the movement between the social classes in this country—both its extent and its processes.[1] The object of these enquiries was to examine more closely than had been possible in the national investigation the ways in which the educational system affects the process of social selection. It was also hoped to throw light on the problems of providing equality of opportunity in post-war English education.

It was important to choose for investigation two areas with the following characteristics: first, each should be large enough to offer an adequate range of educational provision, and should be reasonably self-contained in this respect; secondly, the two should resemble one another in size and educational provision, but should be of contrasting social character in order that post-war educational reform might be seen at work under both favourable and unfavourable conditions.

We looked, therefore, for a prosperous (but not socially homogeneous) area with a population of between 100,000 and 150,000 near London, and then for a comparable but contrasting area in the industrial North of England. The *South West Educational Division of Hertfordshire* conformed to the requirements for the first area, and *Middlesbrough, Yorkshire*, to those for the second. In the case of Middlesbrough there was the additional advantage that a careful

---

[1] cf. Glass, D. V. (ed.) *Social Mobility in Britain.* Kegan Paul, 1954.

survey of local educational provision had already been
made in 1944[1] and could form a basis for the new study.

The work was planned in two stages. First, we were to get
a picture of the social distribution of educational opportunity, and its relation to the distribution of ability in each
area before 1939; this was then to be compared with a
picture of the situation since the passage of the Education
Act in 1944. Parts I and II of this book describe this stage
of the work.[2]

Secondly, the influence of social origins and family
environment, both on children's achievement in various
types of secondary schools and on their subsequent occupations, was to be investigated systematically over a number
of years. This investigation is still in progress. Part III of
this book, however, draws on some of the information
gathered so far. Part IV discusses the social selection underlying academic selection in the grammar schools; this
discussion is based on a study of school records.[3]

II

Before 1944, 'secondary education' was never synonymous
with 'post-primary' education, either in the official or the
public mind. At the beginning of the century there had been
considerable controversy on this matter. On the one side
were those who advocated selecting the ablest children, the
'best brains' of all classes, for admission to the grammar
schools—where they would come into contact with the
national heritage of the 'secondary tradition'. On the other
side were the advocates of an alternative type of post-
primary education, envisaged as a continuation of the public
elementary schools. In 1902, victory went to the supporters

---

[1] cf. Glass, R. (ed.) *Social Background of a Plan: A Survey of
Middlesbrough*. Kegan Paul, 1948.

[2] But the discussion is confined to the case of *boys*, as we were unable
to collect all the information necessary for a comparable analysis of
girls.

[3] Again, in respect of boys only.

of a self-contained secondary school system. Thenceforward for almost half a century, 'equality of educational opportunity' meant the provision of a bridge at the age of 11+ from the 'elementary' to the 'secondary' system, with all that this implied in the way of occupational and social mobility for the small numbers of children involved.

It is true that the Board of Education had declared that the selection of 'the best brains' was not the purpose of the arrangements made in 1907 for a proportion of places in all aided secondary schools to be awarded free to children judged suitable on examination. The intention then was to open the public secondary schools to children of all classes 'as nearly as possible upon equal terms'.[1] But events were to overtake this policy.

The 1920s saw a tremendous public demand for secondary education. This was based on a realistic appreciation of its advantage in the struggle for better jobs and social advancement. The demand was for access to middle-class opportunities, especially to the growing 'new' middle-class of black-coated workers. The continual protests that the secondary schools were producing a nation of clerks were made in vain. The overwhelming majority of parents knew better than to prefer a junior technical to a secondary (grammar) schooling for their children. If their children failed to qualify for free or special places, they showed themselves ready to make great sacrifices to send them to secondary schools as fee-payers. And as is now known, they showed an accurate sense of the distribution of occupational opportunity and prospects.

The national enquiry already mentioned revealed the crucial part played by education in the processes of occupational selection and mobility. It showed that in the years between the wars, the decisive event in the careers of those individuals whose parents were not able to send them to independent schools was their selection or rejection for

---

[1] cf. Glass, D. V. (ed.) op. cit., pp. 104-5, and below, p. 12.

secondary education at the age of 11. For those selected, further education after leaving school could improve their chances of occupational and social mobility; for those rejected, it could only rarely provide adequate compensation. Accordingly it was inevitable that 'equality of educational opportunity' should be firmly established in the public mind, and in large sectors of professional opinion also, as meaning in effect 'equality of economic and social opportunity through education in a secondary school', and that what had been intended as a qualifying examination should be converted into a severe competition for secondary school places.

Official policy, both central and local, made a serious attempt, within the varying limits of available resources, to provide equality of access to the secondary grammar schools.[1] The number of these schools was substantially increased, a growing proportion of places was thrown open to competition, and an immense effort was made to devise objective methods of selection. But the knowledge that social factors frequently infringed the objectivity of these methods created a strong tradition of empirical enquiry—on the one hand into the influence of social factors on the child's chance of succeeding in the selection tests and of being able to accept a free place in a secondary school; and on the other, into the extent of 'social waste' resulting from the failure to match ability, whatever its social origin, with educational opportunity.

Between 1922 and 1939 the reports of H.M. Inspectors on the methods of selecting children for secondary education frequently drew attention to discrepancies in examination results between elementary schools of different social composition. Independent investigators showed the existence and socio-economic basis of a substantial 'refusal rate' for places offered in secondary schools.[2] They analysed the

---

[1] Though the striking regional differences in the distribution of secondary schools are a major source of inequality, this problem has never been successfully tackled.

[2] Lindsay, K., *Educational Progress and Social Waste*. 1926.

economic burden imposed on parents by the payment of fees and the loss of the earnings of children kept at school beyond the age of compulsory attendance.[1] They also demonstrated the influence which material conditions in the primary schools had upon the proportion of successes in the selection examinations.[2]

A beginning was thus made on the task of measuring class inequalities in opportunity. But the social distribution of opportunity could not be estimated with any accuracy or related to the distribution of ability on a national scale. Official sources gave information only of the proportion of those who paid fees to those who held free places, and of those children in the secondary schools who had formerly been pupils in elementary schools to those who had attended private schools. Assumptions could be, and were, made as to the social origins of these groups of children[3] but conclusions based on these assumptions were necessarily only of limited accuracy. An attempt, on the basis of a direct enquiry, to study the relations between the ability and educational opportunity of London school children at various social levels was made by J. L. Gray and Miss P. Moshinsky, working under Professor Hogben in 1934.[4] But the first full account of the social distribution of opportunity up to 1939 on a national scale was provided by the enquiry undertaken in 1949 at the London School of Economics, although it was not possible to relate this to the distribution of ability. For the first time the proportions were given on a national scale of all children of each occupational class who had received secondary schooling. It was thus possible to calculate the chances of a secondary education for children of various classes, and to describe with some accuracy the changes in

---

[1] Leybourne-White, G., *Education and the Birth Rate*. 1940.
[2] Glass, R. (ed.), op. cit.
[3] cf. Hans, N., 'Regional Provision of Secondary Schools, England and Wales': *Year Book of Education*, 1939.
[4] cf. Gray, J. L. and Moshinsky, P., 'Ability and Opportunity in English Education': Hogben, L. (ed.) *Political Arithmetic*, 1938.

the social distribution of educational opportunity which had taken place up to 1939.[1]

It was shown that, despite the expansion of the secondary school system and the greatly increased proportion of pupils who had won total or partial remission of fees in competition, class inequalities in educational opportunity had not been reduced to the extent generally supposed. There were, of course, far more children from families low in the occupational scale entering secondary schools at the end of the period covered by the enquiry than there had been at the beginning; and almost all held free places. Yet their number was still far from proportionate to their strength in the population. The chances of obtaining even a *free* place in a secondary school were shown to be greater at the top of the occupational scale than at the bottom. These facts could be fully explained only if they could be related to the social distribution of intelligence, and if the extent to which social factors influenced the process of selection for secondary education were known. The national investigation, based as it was on a random sample of some 10,000 adults, could provide no information on either point, and there was an obvious need for more intensive studies on a local scale.

The first stage of our enquiry in South West Hertfordshire and Middlesbrough directly follows these earlier investigations. We have examined some of the same ground as former investigators. We have brought up to date in these two areas the account of the social distribution of access to grammar schools, and have related it to the social distribution of ability as measured by intelligence tests. The post-war educational revolution has therefore been documented in the same terms as those in which reform was demanded in the pre-war years.

At the same time, we are aware of the substantial philosophical and educational objections to our definition of

---

[1] cf. Floud, J. E., 'The Educational Experience of the Adult Population', in Glass, D. V. (ed.), op. cit.

equality of educational opportunity. Access to grammar schools is a narrowly conceived criterion of educational success; and the IQ is an arbitrary criterion of ability (in view of the extent to which intelligence tests reflect current educational organization and practice, and measured intelligence represents a set of acquired aptitudes). We have accordingly planned the second stage of the work on broader lines.

The object of the long-term study of the secondary school careers of the children in our samples is to investigate the relations between the home background of children at different social levels, their performance in secondary schools of various types, and their subsequent occupations. Arrangements have been made to record for a period of three years, in the first instance, the school performance and score on an annual intelligence test of those entrants to secondary schools about whom information has already been collected in the first stage of the enquiry. An intensive study will then be made of the home circumstances, past history and further progress to the end of their school course and entry into the labour market, of sub-samples of children who can be identified on various criteria as 'under' or 'over-achievers' respectively in the various types of secondary school. The criteria of 'ability' and of 'opportunity' will, necessarily, be less precise in this part of the work. But it will be possible to take account of at least some aspects of the subtle inter-relations of home and school which determine children's school performance and their later occupations: and to throw light on the features of home environment which influence the educability of children in secondary schools of various types. By this means we shall be able to go at least part of the way to meet readers who may feel dissatisfied with the arbitrary definition in this book of 'opportunity' or 'success' in terms of admission to grammar schools and of 'ability' in terms of measured intelligence.

PART I

SOCIAL STRUCTURE AND
SECONDARY EDUCATION

CHAPTER 1

SOCIAL STRUCTURE AND EDUCATIONAL POLICY IN CONTRASTING AREAS

THE SOCIAL STRUCTURE OF SOUTH WEST HERTFORDSHIRE AND MIDDLESBROUGH, YORKS

South West Hertfordshire is one of the seven administrative districts into which Hertfordshire is divided for educational purposes. It has a population of 155,000, of which 73,000 live in the Borough of Watford and the remainder in four surrounding County Districts—the Urban Districts of Bushey, Rickmansworth and Chorleywood, and the Rural District of Watford. It is that part of the County lying nearest to London, to which fact it owes its rapid development since 1900. It became the resort of professional and business people working in London who wanted a suburban home, and of industries seeking suitable sites for expansion. Since 1900 the population of the Borough of Watford has shown an annual increase of nearly 1,000, but the growth in the other four districts of the Division has been even more rapid, the Rural District of Watford alone having received some 18,000 Londoners to the London County Council housing estate at Oxhey since 1948.

Industry in South West Hertfordshire is light. A wide variety of small and medium sized firms engage in all kinds of manufacture, from biscuits and beer to vehicles and postage stamps. In recent years there has been a notable concentration of the printing and allied trades in the district, and also, though to a lesser extent, of the manufacture of vehicles and precision instruments. The absence of heavy industry and the variety of possible employment has protected the area against severe unemployment, and its

3

social character naturally reflects this favourable picture.
There are in fact few centres in the whole country more
prosperous than Watford.[1]

Nevertheless, although it is an exceptionally prosperous
area inhabited by a higher than average proportion of
professional people, business owners and managers, the
social structure of South West Hertfordshire does not differ
markedly from that of England and Wales as a whole. This
can be judged from the Registrar General's allocation in
1951 of its adult male population into social classes on the
basis of their occupations:

SOCIAL CLASS OF MALES (OCCUPIED AND RETIRED) AGED 15
AND OVER[2]

(PERCENTAGES)

	Managerial	Intermediate	Skilled	Mixed	Unskilled
South West Hertfordshire	6·1	17·1	53·9	12·6	10·3
England and Wales ..	3·3	15·0	52·7	16·2	12·8

The census returns for Hertfordshire as a whole since 1911
show that there has been remarkably little change in the
broad outline of the social and occupational structure of the
county over the past half-century. In particular, the proportions of manual and non-manual workers have scarcely
changed, although it appears that the proportion of unskilled workers may have declined over the period and the

[1] The Marketing Survey Income Levels Index for Watford Borough
is 113. This index is based on the distribution of ownership of cars and
telephones, rateable value per capita, industrial rateable value per
capita, infant mortality and birth rates. It averages 100 for the 145
largest towns in the United Kingdom. Only six of these, Bournemouth,
Eastbourne, Guildford, Hove, Woking and Worthing, have a higher
rating than Watford and none has as high an average rateable value
per head of population. The town with the lowest rating is St. Helens
(87). For Middlesbrough the figure is 92. Cf. Marketing Survey of U.K.,
1951 ed. Chisholm, Cecil, p. 39.

[2] Census of G.B., 1951. 1% Sample Tables and Hertfordshire County
Volume. (Aggregate of figures for Watford M.B., Watford R.D.,
Chorleywood U.D., Rickmansworth U.D. and Bushey U.D.)

proportion of clerical workers has increased at the expense of small shop-keepers and self-employed workers.

In short, South West Hertfordshire is a prosperous but socially differentiated area, well suited to provide the maximum response to post-war measures of social and educational reform.

Middlesbrough offers a striking contrast. With a population of some 146,000, it, too, is a 'new' area, the development of which does not go back for more than a century. But it is a homogeneous community in a sense in which South West Hertfordshire, with its borough and its urban and rural districts, is not. Its prosperity has been spasmodic and largely dependent on the fortunes of the iron and steel industry. Its growth was particularly rapid in the 1870's, when steel superseded iron production and the town, with its natural advantages of situation in relation to raw materials and shipping, became established as a major centre of iron and steel production.

The iron and steel industry has always employed a disproportionate share of the local labour force—in 1911 44·4 per cent., in 1931 39·4 per cent. and in 1952 45 per cent. In addition, chemicals, engineering, shipbuilding and repairing are, or have been, important sources of employment. But there has always been a dearth of light industry, and, on the whole, the other industries found there before 1939 were more or less dependent upon the basic industry. They tended to contract with it in time of difficulty, rather than to complement it or offer opportunities for women to work when their husbands were unemployed.

There was severe unemployment in the area during the depression of the 1930's. Well over 30 per cent. of the insured population of Middlesbrough were out of work in 1932 and the first part of 1933, and it has been suggested that but for local opposition the town would have been officially classed as a 'depressed area'.[1] The contraction of the iron

[1] *The Social Survey of Middlesbrough.* Wartime Social Survey, New Series No. 50, 1945.

and steel industry, which had been under way since the mid-1920's, was intensified in the early 1930's. Middlesbrough was, however, fortunate in being less dependent than neighbouring areas on shipbuilding—which contracted more rapidly and did not recover from the depression with reasonable speed, as the iron and steel industry did, even though at a lower level of output.

Since the recent war the whole of Teeside has been declared a Development Area and two trading estates have been established for light industry, one of them on the eastern boundary of Middlesbrough. However, the dependence of Middlesbrough on heavy industry, and in particular on iron and steel, continues. Post-war reconstruction, export and rearmament created boom conditions so that in 1952 only 1·4 per cent. of the insured population were unemployed. But there can be little doubt that Middlesbrough's post-war prosperity, standing out sharply as it does against the black memories of the inter-war years, is of a very different quality from that of South West Hertfordshire.

The population today is, unlike that of South West Hertfordshire, relatively stable, geographically speaking. It contains an important Catholic minority, mainly of Irish origin, whose strength is not known precisely, although it may be gauged from the fact that some 20 per cent. of the school population in 1953 were drawn from Roman Catholic families. The industrial character of the area makes for an occupational structure which differs from that of South West Hertfordshire notably in the higher proportion of manual to non-manual workers, and in the strength of the group of unskilled workers (see table opposite).

Middlesbrough's main industries are those which employ a large proportion of unskilled labour—metal workers, dock labourers and building workers. In his introductory notes to the North Riding volume of the 1921 Census, the Registrar-General remarks, 'general and undefined labourers are much more numerous in Middlesbrough than in any other County

SOCIAL CLASS OF MALES (OCCUPIED AND RETIRED) AGED 15
AND OVER[1]

PERCENTAGES

	Managerial	Intermediate	Skilled	Mixed	Unskilled
Middlesbrough	1·8	10·8	44·4	18·6	24·4
South West Hertfordshire	6·1	17·1	53·9	12·6	10·3
England and Wales	3·3	15·0	52·7	16·2	12·8

Borough of Yorkshire'.[2] They are for the most part general
labourers attached to the iron and steel 'crews' of skilled and
semi-skilled workers, performing routine heavy manual
work such as iron-ore breaking or ingot-setting. They tend
to form a distinct and socially homogeneous group rather
than a residual and heterogeneous collection of cleaners,
delivery men and casual labourers, scattered over many
industries, as in South West Hertfordshire.

There is in Middlesbrough, therefore, a working-class
which includes a fair-sized Catholic minority and a high
proportion of unskilled workers or general labourers, is
geographically stable and has memories of large-scale
distress and unemployment against which to set present
prosperity. This is in direct contrast with the working-class
in South West Hertfordshire in which skilled workers easily
predominate, which is diverse in its recent geographical
origins and which has a history of steady economic expansion as a background to its present prosperity. Furthermore,
the great majority of the people of Middlesbrough are
manual workers of one sort or another, whereas in South
West Hertfordshire the non-manual occupations are much
better represented.

These differences in the social structure of the two areas
are reflected in the social composition of their school
populations. This is clearly shown by the following comparison of the social origins of children aged 10-11 taking

[1] Census of G.B., 1951. 1% Sample Tables.
[2] Pp. xlii-xliv.

the selection examination for secondary education in the
two areas:

Social Class[1]	South West Hertfordshire (1952)	Middlesbrough (1953)
	%	%
Middle Class[2]	7·0	5·0
Lower Middle Class	26·0	18·0
Working Class	67·0	77·0
	100·0	100·0
	(1,413)	(1,008)*

* This figure represents a 50% sample of the age group.

THE PROVISION OF SECONDARY EDUCATION

In both South West Hertfordshire and Middlesbrough
secondary education is seventy years old. In the former area,
however, it is rooted in a two hundred and fifty year old
tradition of local educational enterprise; the secondary
schools there retained until 1945, at least in modified form,
the independent status which they lost in Middlesbrough as
early as 1900. The two areas also differed markedly in the
generosity with which, before 1944, provision was made for
the award of free places in secondary schools.

In South West Hertfordshire the Watford Grammar
School for boys has developed out of a charity school built
in 1704. Until 1870 this school provided primary education
for 60-70 pupils, the great majority of whom, naturally, did
not pay fees. With the establishment in 1870 of a public
elementary school, however, the old Free School became
redundant, and in 1882 it was reorganized as an Endowed
School, providing mainly a post-primary course for fee-
paying pupils of middle-class origin. Nevertheless it main-

---

[1] Social Class is defined according to the father's occupation. See
p. 150 below.
[2] The strength of this group of children is under-estimated, since
those attending independent schools who did not take the selection
examination are not included.

tained a link with the public elementary school through the tiny body of 'boys and girls of exceptional ability' who were admitted from the elementary schools as 'foundation scholars', or, after 1894, as holders of minor county awards. Up to 1900, boys leaving the Endowed School followed for the most part in the footsteps of their fathers, becoming clerks, engineers and draughtsmen. Towards the end of the century they began to go at the rate of three or four a year to the universities, usually to take degrees in science, and from time to time boys won scholarships to Christ's Hospital. The school attained a high standing among the nation's secondary schools, and in 1902 H.M. Inspector for the area suggested that since the term 'endowed' was associated with elementary education the school should change its name to 'The Watford Grammar School'. The change was made, the school course was extended, and the leaving age raised from 16 to 17.

In Middlesbrough, the High School was founded in 1870 by a group of local industrialists, one of whom gave the site for the school buildings. To meet 'the want of a higher (type of) education than is at present obtainable in Middlesbrough', the industrialists decided to establish a 'school similar to the grammar schools of other towns'.[1] The original intention was that the Trustees should raise an endowment fund which, together with the fees, would enable the school to support itself. But this hope never materialized. The income from fees fluctuated; in hard times children were withdrawn and it was difficult to extract payment of fees from parents. Despite salary cuts, occasional donations from private individuals and grants from the Department of Art and Science and the County Council of the North Riding, the expansion of the school and the extensions to the buildings which were frequently necessary made its existence precarious. Finally in 1897 application had to be made to transfer the school to the Middlesbrough

[1] Circular letter, Mr Hugh Bell, 1870.

Corporation. This was accepted in 1900, when there were some 250 pupils in the boys' school, about one-third of whom did not reside in Middlesbrough itself.

The steadily growing public demand for secondary education which was responsible for, and stimulated by, the passing of the Education Act in 1902, was given further dramatic impetus by the First World War. The extent of this demand was reviewed by the Board of Education in its Annual Report for the year 1923-4:

The great change . . . is the birth and growth of a demand for education; the great problem, what does this demand mean and where does it carry us? We have dealt mainly with schools on the Grant List, but the change does not affect them alone. The Public Schools have experienced it also. Twenty years ago most of them were crying out for pupils, many were in financial difficulties. Now, in spite of high fees, they are full to overflowing, and entry is not easy to secure. The same is true of private schools and of the Universities, especially of the women's colleges. The change does not affect one class but many; the well-to-do manufacturer now gives his son a prolonged education, the artisan and the farm labourer gives his son, or will at least allow him to take, what education he can get.[1]

Both in South West Hertfordshire and in Middlesbrough the demand was felt and considerable efforts were made to meet it. The differences between the areas, in the pace of expansion and in the proportions of the increased numbers of grammar school places which were thrown open to competition, are illustrated in Figures 1 and 2.

In South West Hertfordshire the population grew rapidly. The establishment in 1907 of a higher elementary school, which later became a selective central school, and the slow growth of the Watford Technical School did virtually nothing to mitigate the pressure on the Grammar School. By 1902 there were 180 boys in the Endowed School, and at the end of the war in 1918 the Grammar School, in its new buildings provided with substantial assistance from public

---

[1] 'Some Account of the Recent Development of the Secondary Schools': *Annual Report of the Board of Education for 1923-4.*

Figure 1. PROVISION OF GRAMMAR SCHOOL PLACES FOR BOYS, SOUTH WEST HERTFORDSHIRE (1904-44) AND MIDDLESBROUGH (1905-44)

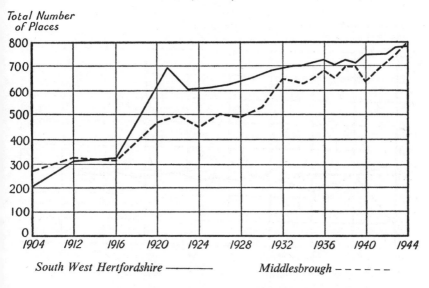

South West Hertfordshire ———— *Middlesbrough* – – – – –

funds, catered for 522 boys. The number of secondary school places had thus multiplied by more than two-and-a-half times—a much faster increase than the general population.

When it came to awarding free places, however, policy remained conservative. Despite capital subventions, the school remained fully independent of the local education authority until 1927, when Direct Grant was relinquished for 'aided' status; only in 1945 was the final encroachment made, when the school became a 'controlled' school within the meaning of the 1944 Act. On several occasions in the decade following the 1907 Regulations the Governors sought in vain for a modification of the rule, which applied to Direct Grant as well as to maintained schools, that the number of free places awarded annually must equal 25 per cent. of the previous year's entry to the school. In 1909 the

Figure 2. PROVISION OF FREE AND SPECIAL PLACES FOR BOYS
IN GRAMMAR SCHOOLS, SOUTH WEST HERTFORDSHIRE (1904-44)
AND MIDDLESBROUGH (1905-44)

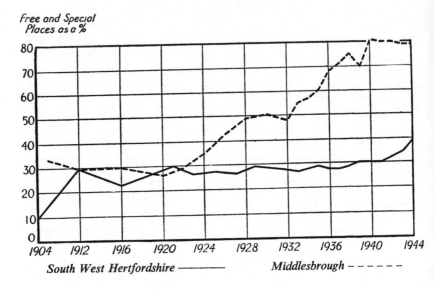

Free and Special
Places as a %

South West Hertfordshire ————   Middlesbrough – – – – –

Board of Education reminded them 'that the object of the
rule . . . is to see that Secondary Schools aided by grants
shall be fully accessible to children of all classes'.[1] Again,
when in 1910 shortage of accommodation restricted the
number in the boys' school to 320, the Governors requested
permission to limit the number of free places to 25 per cent.
of this figure. The Board refused, saying that 'If the accommodation of the school proves insufficient, the number of
fee payers should be limited accordingly.'[2] When the County
Council proposed to reduce the number of County Minor
scholarships and the Governors again asked the Board to

---

[1] Letter to the Governors, 22.6.1909.
[2] Letter to the Governors, 15.6.1910.

sanction a reduction in the number of free places, the Board refused. They added that 'as a matter of principle, the Board are of opinion that the special circumstances created by the war make it more rather than less necessary to maintain the full number of free places in state-aided secondary schools.'[1]

Although this policy resulted in a rise in the proportion of free-place holders, fee-paying pupils predominated in the school right up to the abolition of fees in 1945, and scope for change in its social composition was limited.

In Middlesbrough, too, the provision of secondary school places after 1900 more than kept pace with the growth of the population, although it did not keep pace with the public demand, particularly for places in the boys' school. In 1933 the Education Committee were told that 94 boys had scored 70 per cent. or more of the total marks in the selection tests, but that there were secondary places available for only 64 of them. A second girls' Grammar School had been opened in 1911, but the boys waited until 1935 for a second school.

The pressure on secondary education was partly met in 1922 by re-organizing a Higher Elementary School into a selective Central School with a commercial bias, which from 1933 admitted some 6 per cent. of the secondary age group each year. But the total annual entry to both types of selective secondary school between the wars never amounted to more than 15 per cent. of the age group,[2] although the Junior Technical School, which was organized in 1919 on the basis of the science side of the High School, admitted a further fraction of the secondary age group at 13+, on the recommendation of the Heads of the contributory elementary schools.

By comparison with South West Hertfordshire, Middlesbrough has always been in a certain sense under-provided with places in selective secondary schools, especially con-

---

[1] Letter to the Governors, 10.12.1915.
[2] Annual Reports of Director of Education to Middlesbrough Education Committee.

sidering that a proportion of its selected secondary pupils is
drawn from the North Riding,[1] and that two of its secondary
grammar schools are for Roman Catholic pupils only.
There is no rigidly fixed number of places available in
grammar schools and the number (and the proportion of the
relevant age-group) admitted varies slightly each year.[2] In
1953, when an unusually large number of children reached
the required standard, the proportion was 17 per cent.
(including the Roman Catholic children), as compared with
21·5 per cent. in South West Hertfordshire.

Nevertheless, awards of free places were made on a
generous scale in Middlesbrough, especially after 1921,
when a sub-committee of the Education Committee was
appointed to consider the whole procedure of selection for
transfer from elementary to secondary schools. On its
recommendation the Board of Education was asked in 1922
for permission to increase the number of free places awarded
to more than 25 per cent. of the previous year's entry. In
1929, the Board raised the limit generally to 40 per cent., and
after 1936 abolished it completely. Thus when a new
secondary school for boys was opened in 1935, Middlesbrough was permitted to award free (now 'special') places
in secondary grammar schools up to 60 per cent., and in
1936 up to 80 per cent., of the previous year's entry. By 1938
more than 75 per cent. of the boys in Middlesbrough
grammar schools held free or special places. This liberal
policy obviously gave greater scope for change in the social
composition of the schools than there was in South West
Hertfordshire.

In South West Hertfordshire the grammar school
population increased during the years of the Second World
War, and this increase consisted entirely of special place
pupils. In 1942, the proportion of vacancies available for

[1] The proportion varies from year to year according to the number
of Middlesbrough pupils admitted. In 1953, 39 North Riding pupils
were admitted (15%) and in 1954, 44 (17%).
[2] cf. p. 136 below.

award as special places was raised from 30 to 40 per cent. of the previous year's entry. The procedure of selection was overhauled and its administration was placed in the hands of a Chief Examiner appointed for the County. Since the passage of the 1944 Act there has been a further substantial increase in the provision of grammar school places. In 1950 a new (mixed) grammar school was opened; the selective central school was disbanded and its pupils were transferred to the new school. Another school of the same type was opened in 1953. The grammar schools now cater for some 24 per cent. of the children entering secondary schools each year. The only alternative form of selective secondary education available today is that offered in the technical school, which continues to recruit boys from the modern schools at 13+.[1]

In Middlesbrough, before the passing of the 1944 Act there was no change in the policy of awarding free or special places in secondary schools. In 1939 the number of such places had already stood for two years at 80 per cent. of the previous year's entry. Since 1944, the central schools have not, as in South West Hertfordshire, been absorbed into the grammar schools. They are officially designated 'secondary modern schools', but they remain selective and offer a more broadly based and less intensive course than a secondary grammar school. This course is normally of four years' duration, but may be extended for an optional fifth year during which the examination for the General Certificate of Education may be taken in appropriate subjects.[2] Since 1951 the Technical School has been entered at 11+ through the standard process of selection. A five-year course is offered, and boys successful in the selection tests are given the opportunity to choose the technical school in preference

---

[1] In 1955 the age of entry became 11+.
[2] Thus, since 1950 about one quarter of the annual age-group has remained in school for a fifth year and has taken the G.C.E. examination. A small number of transfers are made to the Sixth Form of a Grammar School.

to a grammar school. Selective secondary education of one sort or another is, therefore, available today for some 26 per cent. of the annual secondary age-group, although the grammar schools themselves admit only some 15-17 per cent.

Thus in the two areas of our study the public system of secondary schools has developed under widely different conditions and there have been marked differences of policy regarding free places in secondary schools. The resulting regional variations in educational opportunity have been of the kind for which the English educational system is notorious. The following chapters will examine their effect in each area on the social composition of the grammar school populations and on the educational fortunes of boys of varying social origins.

CHAPTER 2

THE SOCIAL ORIGINS OF BOYS IN GRAMMAR SCHOOLS BEFORE AND AFTER 1944

SOURCES OF INFORMATION

WE HAVE classified the social origins of grammar school pupils according to the occupations followed by their fathers, which is the only evidence available in respect of past generations of children. Admittedly it is an uncertain guide, especially since fathers' occupations are rarely recorded by the schools in sufficient detail to enable them to be classified with any degree of precision. The Registrar-General's classification of occupations for the purposes of the census, for instance, is the outcome of quite detailed information as to the actual work on which people are engaged, and in the 1951 Census[1] thirteen socio-economic groups are designated. Nothing more was available to us, however, than a brief entry (e.g. the single word 'clerk') in the school admission register, in some cases made forty years ago; our method is therefore rougher and the classification simpler.

We have grouped occupations into five categories under the following headings: professional workers, business owners and managers; clerical workers; foremen, small shop-keepers and other persons in miscellaneous occupations of similar standing; skilled manual workers; unskilled manual workers. To make broader distinctions between the social classes possible, these categories have in some cases,

---

[1] Census of Great Britain, 1951, 1% Sample Tables (Part I, H.M.S.O. 1952).

been combined; thus:—the Middle-Class (professional workers, business owners, managers); the Lower Middle-Class (clerical workers, foremen, small shop-keepers, etc.); and the Working Class (skilled and unskilled manual workers). This classification is based on that used by the Government Social Survey.[1]

It was intended to obtain information about the social origins of entrants to the schools for periods when it might be expected that, under the influence of events or of official policy, the social composition of the schools would be changing. Thus, we were interested (for purposes of comparison) in the years before 1900; in the effects of the introduction of free place awards in 1907, of the First World War, and of the regulations introduced in 1933 under which free places became 'special' places, and the fees payable became dependent upon the means of parents. Unfortunately, it proved impossible to gather extensive and reliable information concerning girls' schools, so that our account of the history of the social composition of the grammar school population is confined in both areas to boys.[2] Neither was it possible to study the same periods of years in the two areas. In the case of South West Hertfordshire the information does not relate to every year in all periods, although in all years for which information was collected a complete census of entrants was taken.[3]

---

[1] See explanatory note, p. 150 below.

[2] For the available information concerning girls in grammar schools in S.W. Hertfordshire see Halsey, A. H., *Education and Social Mobility with special reference to the Grammar School since 1944*, unpublished Ph.D. thesis, University of London, 1954.

[3] The particulars are as follows:

S.W. Hertfordshire		Middlesbrough
1884-1900	(1884-7 inclusive;	1905-18
	1892-4 ,,	1922-30
	1898-1900 ,,)	1935-38
1904-12	(1904-6 inclusive;	
	1910-12 ,,)	
1916-18	(All years)	
1922-30	(1922-4 inclusive;	
	1928-30 ,,)	
1934-8	(1934, 1935 and 1938)	

Information as to the occupations of the fathers of boys entering grammar schools after 1944 is much fuller, since it was obtained by direct enquiry of the parents either in writing or by interview in the course of our investigation into other aspects of the children's home background. Our description of the social distribution of places after 1944 has, therefore, a much sounder basis than our description of their distribution before that date.

'THE EDUCATIONAL LADDER'

In 1885 the occupations of the fathers of boys attending the Watford Grammar School were the subject of an enquiry by the Headmaster, who reported to the Governors that there were in the school at that time:

33 sons of shopkeepers;
22 sons of clerks, commercial travellers and managers;
21 sons of inn and hotel proprietors;
12 sons of auctioneers, civil engineers, teachers and nonconformist ministers;
10 sons of farmers and dealers in corn and cattle;
19 boys with no father living.

Thus the school catered almost exclusively for middle- and lower middle-class boys. The school admission registers[1] show that during the period 1884-1900 about two-thirds of the entrants were sons of clerks and small shopkeepers, and just under one quarter were the sons of professional people, business owners and managers. Only 11 per cent. were the sons of skilled manual workers, and it is interesting to note that as many as three-quarters of these paid fees.

The admission of scholars, even in small numbers, inevitably modified the middle-class character of the school and raised doubts in the minds of the responsible authorities. In 1904, however, the Headmaster reported reassuringly to the Governors:

It will be seen that the number of free scholars from Elementary

---

[1] See Table 1, p. 29, for the social origins of boys entering grammar schools in South West Hertfordshire, 1884-1953.

Schools is eighteen or less than 10 per cent. of the whole school, a proportion which presents no element of difficulty or danger. On the other hand they are picked boys, generally of good ability and they have every incentive to industry. The consequence is that they are amongst our most successful boys.

As a result of the introduction in 1907 of the Board of Education scheme for the award of free places in grant-aided secondary schools to children from elementary schools, the proportion of boys from working-class families rose to 15 per cent. of the total entry in the years 1904-18. But the principal change in the composition of the entry during these years took the form of a redistribution amongst the middle-class groups themselves. Thus, there was a sharp increase in the proportion of sons of business owners, managers and clerical workers mainly at the expense of the sons of foremen and small shop-keepers and, to a much smaller extent, of the sons of professional people. These changes no doubt reflected the changing occupational and residential character of the area.

Although no larger proportion of free places was awarded in the years after the First World War, the expansion of the school resulted in a great increase in the number of free places available. A further rise in the proportion of working-class boys entering the school followed, and during the period 1922-30 such boys made up 19 per cent. of the total entry.

After 1931, however, the world economic depression and consequent measures of educational retrenchment reversed the upward trend in the fortunes of working-class boys, and the period 1934-8 saw the lower middle-class group, which had been losing ground since 1900, restored to something like its former strength. The proportion of boys drawn from the working-class fell from its former peak of just under 20 per cent. in 1922-30 to 16 per cent. in 1934-8, while the proportion of boys of lower middle-class origin rose sharply from 51 per cent. to 62 per cent.

As was mentioned above, changes in the occupational

Figure 3. SOCIAL ORIGINS OF BOYS ENTERING GRAMMAR
SCHOOLS, SOUTH WEST HERTFORDSHIRE (1884-1953)

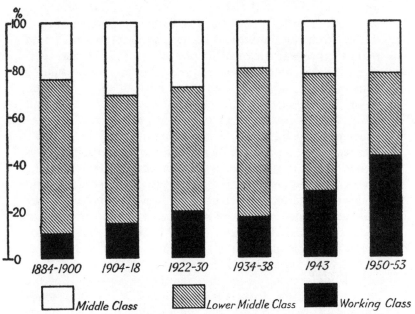

structure of Hertfordshire resulted in a decline in the
importance of small shopkeepers and an influx of clerical
and other black-coated workers into the area. These trends
are reflected in the changing contribution of these groups to
the Boys' Grammar School up to 1930. The sharp decline
during 1934-8 in the proportion of manual workers' sons,
and the rise in the proportion of the sons of clerical workers
entering the school, cannot, however, be attributed to these
gradual changes in the local occupational structure. In the
main they must be attributed to changes in national financial
policy following the depression;[1] the effect of these changes
was to diminish the proportion of places awarded to the
sons of unskilled manual workers.[2]

---

[1] cf. Floud, J. E., op. cit., in Glass, D. V. (ed.), op. cit.
[2] cf. p. 35 below.

The educational fortunes of working-class boys revived during the more prosperous years of the Second World War, and an analysis of the social composition of the entry to grammar schools in 1943 shows that the proportion of boys drawn from the families of manual workers had increased from the pre-war figure of 16 per cent. to 25 per cent. It is interesting to note, however, that these boys were mainly sons of *skilled* workers, and that although the proportion from the unskilled group showed some improvement, it never surpassed their peak proportion of the total entry— 5 per cent.—which had been reached as early as 1922-30. The war also saw a small increase in the proportion of boys drawn from professional and business families. But the lower middle-class group both declined in strength and underwent an internal redistribution which benefited the sons of foremen and small shopkeepers at the expense of those of clerical and other workers. Both these latter trends in the social composition of the school were to be dramatically accentuated after 1944.

In Middlesbrough,[1] the first significant provision for the entry of children from the elementary to the secondary schools was made in 1888 with the founding of fifteen annual scholarships, financed jointly by the Science and Art Department and a local donor. They were tenable on the science side of the High School and were intended for the 'cleverer boys' attending elementary schools. The Scholarships, so the trustees were informed, introduced quite a new class of boys into the school and caused the exodus of a good many others.[2] Ten exhibitioners were sent by the North Riding County Council from 1893 and they too were 'viewed with distrust in many quarters'. The 'number of middle-class boys fell still further', and for several terms

---

[1] The social origins of boys entering Roman Catholic grammar schools are discussed separately. See p. 134 below.

[2] 'History of Middlesbrough High School and the Science School, 1870-1919.' Report printed for subscribers by the Trustees.

following the admission of elementary school boys, 'the school suffered severely in consequence by the withdrawal of boys who were sent to boarding schools'. However, the Headmaster was able to report that 'the tone of the school (had) not suffered in the least', and although scholarships were restricted to those whose parents' income did not exceed £200, 'they would be drawn from respectable families in which the moral tone would be high and the proper bringing up of the children a matter of anxiety to the parents'.[1] In fact, the quality of the work in the school rose, 'the fee-payers benefited', and middle-class parents were asked to 'reconcile themselves to what was happening' and to recognize the advantage of educating the working-classes.[2] But there was an unfavourable side to this otherwise generally satisfactory picture as the Headmaster revealed in his annual report for 1896. In the last eight years, he reported, one hundred and sixty scholars 'whose mental development in many cases is marvellous', had been admitted from elementary schools. 'But', he went on, 'I cannot forbear expressing my deep regret that no suitable careers appear open to these youths. Up to, say, 17 they receive an education well fitted to modern requirements . . . (but) . . . we have no means of placing them in business or sending them forward to a University—and in far too many instances, after waiting—and deteriorating—for months, they are glad to fall in with situations far below their merits. I look upon this as so much national loss and waste of

---

[1] The occupations followed by the fathers of the first fifteen holders of Science and Art scholarships in 1888 at the Boys' High School are given as follows in the Minutes of the High School Trustees:

Skilled Manual	10
Labourer	1
Small shopkeeper	3
Minor Clerical	1
	15

[2] 'History of Middlesbrough High School, etc.'

ability, and although it is not my province to indicate any means of cure, yet I am convinced that something will have to be done to utilize for our country's benefit—if only to hold our own in competition with the foreigner—those abundant stores of mental power which at present are so neglected.'[1]

As might be expected from a more liberal policy in awarding free places, there was a steady increase in the proportion of working-class boys admitted annually to the secondary schools in Middlesbrough.[2] In 1935 a second boys' grammar school was opened and the award of still more free or special places was accompanied by an attempt, which was largely successful, to see that the entire age-group of eligible children took the preliminary selection tests.[3] There was no decline after 1935 in the proportion of entrants of working-class origin such as took place in South West Hertfordshire, and the sons of manual workers increased their proportion of the total entry from 38 per cent. in 1922-30 to 46 per cent. in 1935-8. By this time the sons of *non-manual* workers (as can be seen from Figure 4 below) accounted for only a little over half the entry, and only the sons of clerical workers had improved their position. The proportion of boys from professional and business families, and especially the sons of foremen and small shopkeepers, declined steadily throughout the period up to 1938.

The effect which the economic depression and the Special Place Regulations clearly produced on the composition of the entry in South West Hertfordshire was not so evident in Middlesbrough because of the larger number of places thrown open to competition. This sustained the working-class

---

[1] Headmaster's Report, 1896.
[2] See Table 2, p. 30, for the social origins of boys entering grammar schools in Middlesbrough, 1905-53.
[3] In 1943, 93% of the age group took the tests. However, the proportion varied widely between districts of the town according to their prosperity. Schools in the poorest districts showed a turn-out of only 85% as compared with 99% in the more prosperous residential areas outside the centre. Cf. Glass, R., op. cit., p. 128.

Figure 4. SOCIAL ORIGINS OF BOYS ENTERING GRAMMAR
SCHOOLS, MIDDLESBROUGH (1905-53) (1)

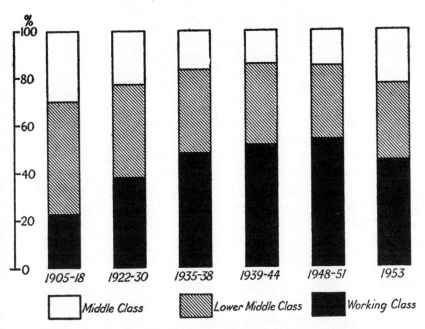

(1) *Excluding Boys entering Roman Catholic Grammar Schools*

contribution to the total entry despite a fairly steep
fall in the *proportion of awards* to the sons of skilled workers.[1]
We can only speculate as to what effect the increase in the
proportion of free places might have had under more
favourable economic conditions. When the war years

---

[1] See p. 36 below. It is difficult to account for this decline in the
competitive position of skilled workers' children in Middlesbrough,
which is in direct contrast to the position in South West Hertfordshire,
where the brunt of the depression was borne by boys from unskilled
workers' families. It is possible that the depression in Middlesbrough
was felt more keenly by skilled workers in the shipbuilding industry
than by unskilled workers mainly employed in the steel industry which
was not so badly hit.

brought full employment there was an increase in the proportion of both skilled and unskilled workers' sons entering the grammar schools; the working-class group in the entry as a whole increased from 46 per cent. in 1935-8 to 52 per cent. in 1939-44. It seems, however, that this was caused by an increase in the proportion of working-class fee-payers as well as by an improvement in the competitive strength of these boys.[1]

'SECONDARY EDUCATION FOR ALL'

In 1945 fees were abolished in all maintained and aided schools, and in both areas the result has been that an increased proportion of working-class boys have entered the grammar schools. This increase has, of course, been more striking in South West Hertfordshire than in Middlesbrough, where even before 1944 over half the entry was drawn from the working-class.

In Middlesbrough, the balance of the distribution of the total entry of boys to the grammar schools as between the sons of non-manual and of manual workers has moved slightly since 1945 in favour of the latter groups. The change has, however, been insignificant.

In South West Hertfordshire a number of special circumstances were responsible for a series of fluctuations in the composition of the grammar school entry after 1945. Strangely enough, the immediate result of the abolition of fees was a sharp reduction in the intake of working-class boys. This was probably due, however, to the admission of a large number of intending fee-payers from the preparatory department of the school. During the years 1946-9 there appeared to be a 'flight' of middle-class boys from the school; and the opening in 1950 of the new mixed grammar school at Bushey, which admitted many working-class children

---

[1] This question of the competitive strength of the social classes is complicated by its relationship to the social distribution of intelligence, and is discussed in greater detail, pp. 44-53 below.

from the expanding L.C.C. housing estate at Oxhey, lowered still further the representation of the middle-class in the total grammar school entry. Since 1950, however, the middle-class group has regained its former strength and now contributes more than 20 per cent. of the entry. But the lower middle-class group of boys from the families of clerical, supervisory and self-employed workers has continued to lose ground, and their proportion has fallen from about two-thirds in pre-war years to a figure nearer one-third in 1950-2. Their place as tne largest of the occupational groups has been taken by the sons of manual workers.

It is not surprising that in the many areas of the country which have a social structure and educational history similar to that of South West Hertfordshire, the frustration of an earnest and ambitious body of parents is widely advertised. Nor is it surprising that the schools themselves are worried by the problems which the new conditions have created. Disquiet[1] today replaces the equanimity, and indeed enthusiasm, with which the nineteenth-century headmasters welcomed their able recruits from the elementary schools and attempted to allay the fears of middle-class parents.

Table 3 (p. 28) shows the social origins of the boys attending the grammar schools in these two areas during the years of our enquiry. This picture of the position after a decade of 'secondary education for all' illustrates the cumulative effects not only of the distribution of opportunity at the moment of entry to the schools, but of a process of social selection going on within them. Working-class

[1] 'The grammar school now includes among its pupils a much higher proportion of children from poorer homes. Some of these children come from homes which are barely literate and where a book is an unusual phenomenon . . . Others have very low standards of cleanliness and appearance; some seem to have had very little training in social behaviour; even table manners may leave much to be desired. Children like these have very little to give to the social or cultural life of the school; the school itself has to provide much which, before the war, would have been regarded as the normal contribution of the home'. Davies, H., 'The Social Effects of the 1944 Act on the Grammar School.' *The Bulletin of Education*, No. 23, Nov. 1950, p. 5.

children tend to leave early rather than late, and are under-represented in the upper forms of the schools. The distribution of opportunity and this process of internal selection in the grammar schools is examined more closely in the chapters which follow.

Table 3

SOCIAL ORIGINS OF BOYS ATTENDING GRAMMAR SCHOOLS, SOUTH WEST HERTFORDSHIRE (1952) AND MIDDLESBROUGH (1953)

Father's Occupation	South West Hertfordshire (1952) %	Middlesbrough* (1953) %
Professional workers and business owners and managers	21·6	11·6
Clerical workers	16·2	13·3
Foremen, small shop-keepers, and other similar grades	21·2	21·2
Skilled manual workers	30·5	25·8
Unskilled manual workers	5·9	16·6
Unclassified	4·6	12·5
Total ..	100·0	100·0
(N)	718	774

* *Excluding boys attending Roman Catholic grammar schools.*

Table 1

SOCIAL ORIGINS OF BOYS ENTERING GRAMMAR SCHOOLS. SOUTH WEST HERTFORDSHIRE, 1884-1953

Father's Occupation	1884-1900 %	1904-1918 %	1922-1930 %	1934-38 %	1943 %	1950-1953 %
Professional workers and business owners and managers	23·8	31·3	27·6	19·1	23·0	21·0
Clerical workers	16·6	23·8	21·0	32·5	23·8	16·0
Foremen, small shopkeepers and other similar grades	48·4	30·4	30·3	29·0	25·4	19·0
Skilled manual workers	10·8	12·8	14·6	12·8	20·6	34·0
Unskilled manual workers	0·4	1·7	4·7	3·3	4·8	8·0
Unclassified[1]	0·0	0·0	1·8	3·3	2·4	2·0
Total	100·0	100·0	100·0	100·0	100·0	100·0
(N)	517	873	694	366	126	639

[1] When preparing summary figures for presentation in diagrammatic form (*see Figure 3. p. 21 above*) the numbers in this category were redistributed proportionately among the occupational groups.

Table 2

SOCIAL ORIGINS OF BOYS ENTERING GRAMMAR SCHOOLS.[1] MIDDLESBROUGH, 1905-1953

Father's Occupation	1905-1918 %	1922-1930 %	1935-1938 %	1939-1944 %	1948-1951 %	1953 %
Professional workers and business owners and managers	29·8	22·8	16·1	13·9	15·4	23·3
Clerical workers	7·8	7·6	15·2	15·7	12·6	7·7
Foremen, small shopkeepers, and other similar grades ..	38·6	30·5	18·6	18·1	18·0	24·4
Skilled manual workers ..	16·2	27·0	29·5	33·7	31·6	30·8
Unskilled manual workers ..	6·6	10·5	16·1	18·6	22·4	13·8
Unclassified[2]	1·0	1·6	4·5	—[3]	—	—
Total	100·0	100·0	100·0	100·0	100·0	100·0
(N)	993	811	575	888	556	148

[1] Excluding those entering Roman Catholic Grammar Schools, of which an account is given separately (see p. 134, below).

[2] When preparing summary figures for presentation in diagrammatic form (see Figure 4, p. 25 above) the numbers in this category were distributed proportionately among the occupational groups.

[3] In this period the occupations of an unusually large proportion (11%) of fathers could not be classified since they were recorded simply as 'Army'. The numbers have been distributed proportionately among the occupational groups.

PART II

OPPORTUNITY, ABILITY, AND SOCIAL
CLASS

PART II

THE account which has been given of changes in the social composition of the grammar schools tells us very little about the distribution of educational opportunity—that is to say, about the likelihood that a child from a particular social class will be admitted to a grammar school. This likelihood cannot be deduced from the number of children admitted to the grammar schools from each social class; we must also know the total number of children in each social class qualified by age to be admitted. A large number of working-class boys, for instance, may enter the grammar schools and may constitute a sizeable fraction of the total intake; but if it represents only a tiny minority of the age-group of working-class boys from which it is drawn, the probability or 'chance' that a son of working-class parents will reach a grammar school remains small. Today we see working-class boys entering the grammar schools in greater numbers and forming a much larger group in the population of these schools than ever before. Yet, judging by the post-war situation in South West Hertfordshire and Middlesbrough, the likelihood that a working-class boy will reach a grammar school is not notably greater today, despite all the changes, than it was before 1945. Rather less than 10 per cent. of working-class boys reaching the age of 11 in the years 1931-41 entered selective secondary schools.[1] In 1953 in South West Hertfordshire the proportion was $15 \cdot 5$ per cent. and in Middlesbrough, 12 per cent.

The distribution of opportunity must also be related to ability. If an IQ of, say, 115 represents the minimum intellectual qualification for entry to a grammar school, we must also ask whether the full quota of children at or above this level of measured intelligence from every social

---

[1] cf. Glass, D. V. (ed.), op. cit., Chapter V.

class is admitted—or whether the position is like that in London in 1933-4, when it was found that less than one-quarter of the children with an IQ of 130 or more whose fathers were unskilled workers, and only about one-third of those whose parents were skilled workers, went to secondary schools.

The discussion of these problems will begin with an account in Chapter 3 of the history of the social distribution of awards of free and special places; against this background we can then examine, in Chapter 4, the social distribution of opportunity and its relation to ability under present-day conditions of full competition.

THE SOCIAL DISTRIBUTION OF AWARDS OF FREE AND SPECIAL PLACES IN GRAMMAR SCHOOLS

THE increasing number of places open to competition and the proportion of awards to boys in each of the social classes at various times over the past half century are set out in Table 4, p. 40, and illustrated in Figure 5.

The striking feature of both areas is the reversal after 1930 of the earlier upward trend in the competitive fortunes of working-class boys. This can be attributed in part to the impact of the world economic depression and to the measures of educational retrenchment which followed. In 1933 the Board, upon the recommendations of the May Committee on Public Expenditure, decided to economize by increasing school fees and lowering the income level below which maintenance grants were to be given to children remaining at school beyond the age of compulsory attendance. The Board also introduced Special Place Regulations under which places awarded in competition were assessed for fees according to parents' means. Subsequently the proportion of places awarded to working-class boys declined.

In South West Hertfordshire working-class boys were awarded 56 per cent. of the available free places during 1922-30, but in 1934-38 their share dropped to 48 per cent. This reduction was entirely at the expense of the sons of *unskilled* workers. Their proportion of free or special places was almost halved in the period 1934-38, whereas that of the sons of *skilled* manual workers remained unchanged. In Middlesbrough, the number of places open to competition was greatly increased after 1935, but the proportion awarded

to the sons of manual workers fell from 63 per cent. in
1922-30 to 53 per cent. in 1935-38. In both areas the sons of
clerical workers substantially improved their competitive
strength. In South West Hertfordshire they increased their
share of free places by nearly 50 per cent., gaining 22 per
cent. of those available in 1934-39 as against only 16 per cent.
in 1922-30, and in Middlesbrough they almost trebled their
awards (from 5 per cent., 1922-30, to 14 per cent., 1935-38).

The economic situation had stiffened the terms of
competition for working-class children. Economic difficulties in the home may well have increased their tendency
either to refuse the offer of a place in a grammar school
outright, or to accept the alternative of a place at a central
school, which had a shorter course and perhaps a more
practical bias.[1] Financial difficulties in the 1930's also
induced many lower middle-class parents to send their
children to the public elementary schools. These children
tended on the average to be of slightly higher ability than
those from working-class families, but even those of the
same level of ability were often in a better position to profit
from teaching directed towards the selection examination.
The competition was in any case gradually opened to
private as well as public elementary schools.

Nevertheless, after 1933 the number of places available
for award was greatly increased in both areas and, other
things being equal, it might have been expected that working-
class boys would continue to secure at least the same, if not
an increased proportion of places. Yet the decline in competitive strength had set in and the ground lost was never
regained, even under more favourable economic conditions
and with all places open to award.

When fees were abolished in 1945 the process, long since

---

[1] It is perhaps significant that the first mention of such refusals in
the Minutes of the Governors of the Grammar School in South West
Hertfordshire occurs in 1934. Between 1934 and 1938 7% of free and
special places offered were refused—for the most part in favour of a
place at the Central School.

Figure 5. SOCIAL DISTRIBUTION OF FREE AND SPECIAL PLACES

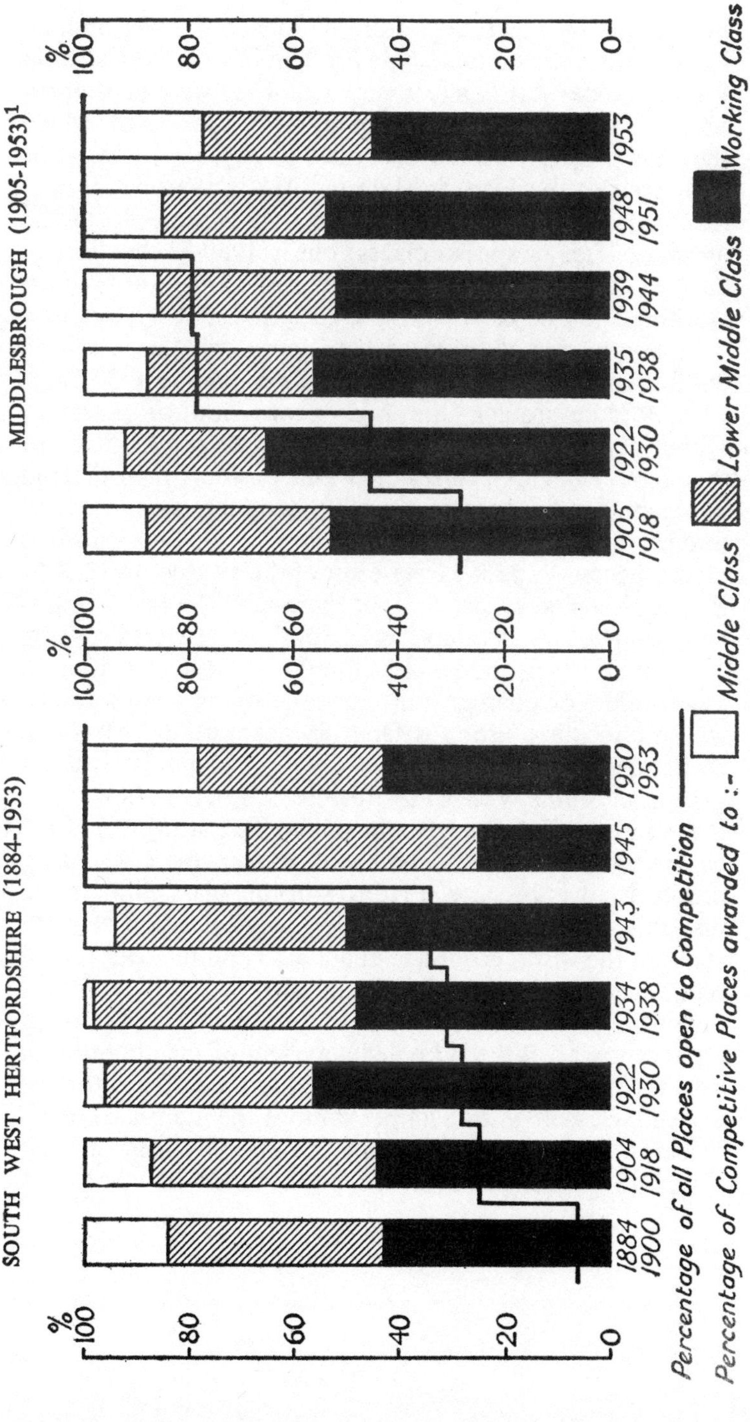
SOUTH WEST HERTFORDSHIRE (1884-1953)
MIDDLESBROUGH (1905-1953)[1]
%
100
80
60
40
20
0
1884 1900
1904 1918
1922 1930
1934 1938
1943
1945
1950 1953
1905 1918
1922 1930
1935 1938
1939 1944
1948 1951
1953
Percentage of all Places open to Competition
Percentage of Competitive Places awarded to :-
Middle Class
Lower Middle Class
Working Class

[1] Excluding places in Roman Catholic Grammar Schools.

under way, by which boys from middle- and lower middle-class families were increasingly brought into the competition for free places was finally completed. They were henceforth obliged to compete for places in grammar schools for which they had formerly been accustomed to pay.

In South West Hertfordshire in 1934-38 the sons of professional and business men gained only 2 per cent. of the awards of free or special places; but in 1950-52 they gained 20 per cent. of the places. The proportion awarded to working-class boys was only slightly reduced by this new competition, but that awarded to lower middle-class boys fell from a pre-war 49 per cent. to 33 per cent. in 1950-52.

In Middlesbrough, the high proportion of grammar school places open to competition even before 1945 meant that fewer sons of professional and business men entered as fee-payers, and more than 60 per cent. of their total number in the grammar school entry in 1939-44 held free places, accounting for 11 per cent. of the awards. In 1948-51 they represented 15 per cent. of the entry. The losers in this new competition were not, as in South West Hertfordshire, the sons of lower middle-class families (whose allocation of places did not change) but the sons of manual workers, whose allocation dropped from 58 per cent. in 1939-44 to 54 per cent. in 1948-51.

Both in South West Hertfordshire and in Middlesbrough the number of free places has been increasing since the beginning of the 1930's. But with each increase a smaller proportion has been awarded to working-class children. At first this weakening of their competitive position was the result of the world economic depression and the educational economies introduced in 1933, and there was some recovery in South West Hertfordshire during the prosperous years of the recent war. But the immediate effect of the abolition of fees was to reinforce the downward trend, for although working-class boys won 44 per cent. of the grammar school places in 1950-52 this represents no improvement on their competitive strength over the period 1934-38 when they

were awarded 40 per cent. of the available free places. On
the contrary, their virtually unchanged proportion of a
greatly expanded number of free places represents, in effect,
a relative weakening of their competitive position.

The son of non-manual workers has not only always had
a better general chance of obtaining entry to a grammar
school, but his chances of doing so *as a holder of a free place*
have improved with each fresh increase in the number of
places thrown open to competition. When working-class
boys have obtained entry to the grammar schools they
have done so in overwhelming proportion as free place
holders, but successive increases in the number of places
open to competition have failed to improve their chances in
proportion. Under conditions of 'full competition', and the
provision of places being what it is at present, there is, in
effect, a limit to the expansion of their chances of a secondary grammar school education despite their numerical
preponderance in the general population. Neither in South
West Hertfordshire, where manual workers form some 65
per cent. of the occupied population, nor in Middlesbrough,
where they form as much as 85 per cent., do their sons
represent more than 45-50 per cent. of the annual entry of
boys to the grammar schools.

It is true that, if we compare the social composition of the
age-group[1] with that of the grammar school intake, there is a
marked difference between the two areas in the extent to which
the working-class is 'under-represented', and other social
groups are 'over-represented' in the grammar school entry.
The 'better' representation of the working- and lower
middle-class groups in the South West Hertfordshire entry
can be attributed partly to the greater number of grammar
school places there, and partly to less severe competition
from the sons of professional and business men who,
though they constitute a larger proportion of the whole
population than in Middlesbrough, presumably make
greater use of independent schools.

[1] See p. 8 above.

Table 4

SOCIAL ORIGINS OF BOYS ENTERING GRAMMAR SCHOOLS WITH FREE AND SPECIAL PLACES, SOUTH WEST HERTFORDSHIRE, 1884-1953

Father's Occupation	1884-1900 %	1904-1918 %	1922-1930 %	1934-1938 %	1943 %	1950-1953 %
Professional workers and business owners and managers	16	13	4	2	5	21
Clerical workers	34	19	16	22	21	16
Foremen, small shopkeepers, and other grades	6	24	24	27	21	19
Skilled manual workers	44	37	39	38	33	34
Unskilled manual workers	0	7	17	10	14	8
Unclassified	0	0	0	1	6	2
Total	100	100	100	100	100	100
(N)	32	215	196	113	43	639

Table 5

SOCIAL ORIGINS OF BOYS ENTERING GRAMMAR SCHOOLS[1] WITH FREE AND SPECIAL PLACES,
MIDDLESBROUGH, 1905-1953

Father's Occupation	1905-1918 %	1922-1930 %	1935-1938 %	1948-1951 %	1953 %
Professional workers and business owners and managers	12	8	12	15	23
Clerical workers	8	5	14	13	8
Foremen, small shopkeepers, etc.	26	21	16	18	24
Skilled manual workers	38	43	34	32	31
Unskilled manual workers	14	20	19	22	14
Unclassified[2]	2	3	5	3	—
Total	100	100	100	100	100
(N)	279	361	446	556	148

[1] Excluding those entering Roman Catholic Grammar Schools, of which an account is given separately (see p. 134, below.

[2] When preparing summary figures for presentation in diagrammatic form (see Figure 4, p. 25 above) the numbers in this category were distributed proportionately among the occupational groups.

[3] In this period the occupations of an unusually large proportion (11%) of fathers could not be classified since they were recorded simply as 'Army'. The numbers have been distributed proportionately among the occupational groups.

CHAPTER 4

SOCIAL CLASS AND CHANCES OF ADMISSION TO GRAMMAR SCHOOLS

'CLASS CHANCES'

THE proportions of the 10-11 age-group of children in each occupational group selected for admission to grammar schools give what may be called the 'class-chances' of a grammar school education.

The following are the figures for boys in 1953 in South West Hertfordshire and Middlesbrough:[1]

	South West Hertfordshire %	Middlesbrough %
Professional workers, business owners and managers	59	68
Clerical workers	44	37
Foremen, small shopkeepers, etc. ..	30	24
Skilled manual workers	18	14
Unskilled manual workers	9	9
All	22	17

As might be expected, there were in both areas consider-able disparities in the chances of boys from different social classes. In general, the sons of manual workers had a chance below the average, and the sons of non-manual workers a chance above the average, of being selected for grammar schools. The sons of clerks had four or more times as good a chance as the sons of unskilled manual workers, and two to three times the chance of sons of skilled workers. The differ-ence in chances at the extremes of the occupational scale was still greater. In Middlesbrough the son of a professional

---

[1] In this chapter the Middlesbrough figures include children of Roman Catholic families.

or business man had more than seven times the chance of the son of an unskilled worker, and almost five times the chance of a skilled worker's son, while in South West Hertfordshire he had three times the chance of the skilled worker's and six times that of the unskilled worker's son.[1]

'Class chances' vary from year to year, however. For example, in South West Hertfordshire they have varied for boys over three years as follows:[2]

	1952 %	1953 %	1954 %
Professional workers, business owners and managers	40	59	64
Clerical workers	35	44	46
Foremen, small shopkeepers, etc. ..	21	30	32
Skilled and unskilled manual workers	15	14	12

If the chances of working-class boys diminish over a period of years—i.e., if a smaller proportion of the particular age-group at this social level is admitted to the grammar schools—does this mean that working-class boys of appropriate ability are being excluded? Or have the terms of competition turned against them? Are there proportionately fewer grammar school places available (say, because the numbers in the 10-11 age-group have increased without a corresponding expansion of the grammar school intake)? Is the competition from middle-class children of higher average IQ more intense than formerly (say, because of a change in the social composition of the age-group, or because middle-class parents are turning in increasing numbers away from independent to grammar schools)?

'Class chances' depend on several factors: on the number of grammar school places, on the proportion of them open to competition and the qualifying conditions for competing, and on the size and the social and intellectual composition

---

[1] These disparities are underestimated, of course, since no account has been taken of the use made of independent schools.

[2] The figures for 1953 and 1954 have been calculated from information which the Heads of schools and the Divisional Education Officer kindly supplied.

of the age-group of children from which entrants are drawn. To calculate class chances precisely and relate them to ability, information is needed on all these points—and is rarely available. We were, in fact, able to assemble it accurately only in respect of grant-earning schools and for the single years of our enquiry. As regards other years, although we have collected information about the provision and social distribution of places in grant-aided schools, we know nothing about the social distribution of intelligence; and we can only estimate changes in the size and social composition of the age-group from the information available in census returns from the two areas as to the numbers of children of 10-14 and the social composition of the general population. Precise calculations of class chances and their relation to ability cannot, therefore, be made except for the years 1952 in South West Hertfordshire and 1953 in Middlesbrough. Nevertheless, we decided to make estimates for other years with the aid of a simplified model based on the available data for these years and on the assumption that the size and social and intellectual composition of the age-group are constant. The error to which the calculations based on this assumption give rise, so far as it can be assessed, and the general limitations of the method will be made clear in the course of the following discussion.

'CLASS CHANCES' AND MEASURED INTELLIGENCE

The broad facts of the social distribution of measured intelligence are well-known. Capacity to score in intelligence tests improves with social level, but the differences within occupational groups are greater than those between them. Thus, the mean IQ of the highest occupational group was greater by 15 to 20 points than that of the lowest, both in South West Hertfordshire in 1952 and in Middlesbrough in 1953, but the range of IQ within the groups overlapped between them to a considerable extent.[1]

---

[1] cf. Table 6, p. 59.

Figure 6.

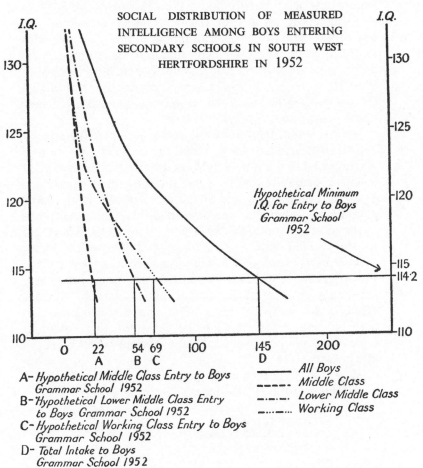

SOCIAL DISTRIBUTION OF MEASURED INTELLIGENCE AMONG BOYS ENTERING SECONDARY SCHOOLS IN SOUTH WEST HERTFORDSHIRE IN 1952

A- Hypothetical Middle Class Entry to Boys
    Grammar School 1952
B- Hypothetical Lower Middle Class Entry
    to Boys Grammar School 1952
C- Hypothetical Working Class Entry to Boys
    Grammar School 1952
D- Total Intake to Boys
    Grammar School 1952

——— All Boys
- - - - Middle Class
—·—·— Lower Middle Class
—··—··— Working Class

The problem is to assess the relevance of these facts to the ability of children at each social level to compete with others for entry to grammar schools at any given level of provision of places.

The Intelligence Quotients of the boys aged 10-11 who

provide our samples[1] can be plotted cumulatively, as in Figure 6, which relates to South West Hertfordshire in 1952. A given point on any of the curves then shows on the horizontal scale the number of children in our sample with an IQ equal to, or greater than, that indicated at the corresponding point on the vertical scale. For instance, in South West Hertfordshire in 1952 at and above the IQ level of 125, there were 43 boys, 10 of whom were middle-class, 26 lower middle-class, and 13 working-class.

We know that there were 145 places available for boys in 1952. It is possible to deduce what the social composition of a group of 145 entrants would be, were the places awarded solely according to ability as measured by intelligence tests. The point at which a line at the number 145 on the horizontal scale intersects the curve describing the intelligence of the total age-group can be seen in Figure 6 to correspond on the vertical scale to an IQ of 114·2. This is the hypothetical minimum level of ability required to obtain a place in a grammar school in 1952. The distribution of the entry among the three social classes that would have resulted from selection solely on the basis of measured intelligence can then be obtained by reading the values on the horizontal scale of the points at which the appropriate curves meet the line drawn at 114·2 IQ.

Thus the hypothetically 'perfect' or 'expected' social distribution of the 1952 entry is as follows:

			N	%
Middle-Class	..	..	22	15
Lower Middle-Class	..		54	37
Working-Class	..	..	69	48
			145	100

---

[1] In South West Hertfordshire (1952) 710 boys, in Middlesbrough (1953) 752 (this latter figure being twice the number in our 50% sample of the age-group). It should be noted that the samples included only those children who took part in the selection procedure and that an unknown but not necessarily insignificant proportion of children of middle-class origin were therefore excluded.

This may be compared with the *actual* distribution of the 1952 entry which was:

	N	%
Middle-Class	22	15
Lower Middle-Class ..	49	34
Working-Class	74	51
	145	100

The model has been used to make these calculations for each area in respect, firstly, of the annual intake of boys holding free and special places (Table 7, p. 60), and secondly, of the total annual entry of boys at various periods between 1904 and 1952 (Table 8, p. 61). The degree of error in the assumptions on which it is based as to the size and the social and intellectual composition of the age-group cannot be accurately assessed. The size of the age-group has obviously fluctuated with changes in birth-rates and movements of population, but it has certainly not increased at the same rate as the general population. The general population of both areas has increased since 1900; it has trebled in South West Hertfordshire and increased by some 37 per cent. in Middlesbrough. But it has been ageing, and the number of children between the ages of 10-14 has increased much less rapidly—by only 63 per cent. in South West Hertfordshire and 14 per cent. in Middlesbrough. The social class structure in both areas has remained only roughly constant; on balance, there has probably been some shrinkage in the proportion of manual to non-manual workers, and within the latter group, an increase in the proportion of clerical workers as against small shopkeepers and self-employed workers. These changes in the social composition of the general population would be more marked in the case of the 10-11 year age-group as a result of class differences in birth rates. Nothing is known about the changes in the social distribution of intelligence, but there is no reason *prima facie* to suppose that it has not in fact remained constant as we have assumed.

Nevertheless, though the model is simplified, it does

enable us to estimate in approximate terms the part played by the social distribution of measured intelligence in the long-term decline in the competitive capacity of working-class children[1] and the extent to which 'ability' and 'opportunity' are more closely related today than when J. L. Gray and Miss Moshinsky demonstrated discrepancies in the 1930's.[2]

SOCIAL CLASS AND COMPETITION FOR FREE AND SPECIAL PLACES

Column 8 of Table 7 (p. 60) shows the increase in the annual provision of free and special places, which, on the assumption that the age-group is constant in size, is reflected in the fall shown in column 1 in the minimum IQ necessary to obtain a place in competition. In fact, the age-group increased over the period covered by the table in both areas, but the increase in the number of free and special places easily outstripped it, and the decline in the minimum IQ is not seriously exaggerated in column 1. Graph readings presented in percentage form in columns 2, 4 and 6 show the proportions in which the social classes would have been represented in the competitive entry at each point of time, had the competition been open to all and had all competed. The social composition of the age-group is assumed to be constant. In fact, the proportion of working-class children in the age-group probably decreased over the period covered by the table, so that the discrepancy between the expected and the actual proportions of free places awarded to working-class boys (columns 6 and 7) is probably slightly under-estimated for the years before 1945. That is to say, the proportion of awards which working-class children would be expected to win in open competition on the basis of measured intelligence alone was probably lower than is shown in column 6 for the pre-1945 years, and the terms of

---

[1] See p. 38 above.
[2] See p. 51 below.

competition before 1945 were probably even more in their favour than the figures suggest.

The distribution of intelligence is such that had the competition been open to all, and had all competed, the proportion of the available awards won by working-class boys would have increased with every increase in the number of places open to competition, whilst that of awards to middle-class, and later also to lower middle-class, boys would have fallen (columns 2, 4 and 6).[1] In fact, columns 3, 5 and 7 show the opposite trend.

Middle-class children who attended private schools were for long excluded from the competition, and right up to 1945 they entered the schools as fee-payers more or less without regard to their ability. Working-class children were to that extent 'protected' in the competition, and won a correspondingly greater proportion of the available free and special places. (It need hardly be pointed out that the effect of their advantage on the general relation of ability to opportunity was far outweighed by the alternatives open to children in other social groups.)

In South West Hertfordshire working-class boys competed on very favourable terms for a limited number of free places right up to 1945; middle-class boys hardly competed at all. In the 1930's lower middle-class boys benefited from middle-class abstention, gaining a slightly higher proportion of free or special places than would have been awarded to them solely on grounds of their relative ability. But the greatest gain went to the working-class boys, who, in terms of their relative ability, were consistently over-represented—though to a diminishing extent—in the group of free and special

---

[1] This trend would continue up to the point where selection for secondary education was abandoned, But the *chances* of working-class boys would, of course, only be equal to those of others in this limiting case. So long as children are selected by competitive examination for a number of school places which is smaller than the number of candidates in the age-group, the classes (differences in their respective size notwithstanding) are bound to have varying chances of admission according to their average level of measured intelligence.

place pupils. In 1945 their position was suddenly and dramatically reversed; this reverse was only temporary however, and was probably the result of the admission, under the special circumstances of the sudden abolition of fees, of a large number of intending fee-payers from the preparatory department of the grammar school. In 1952, the year of our enquiry in the area, the relationship between 'ability' and 'opportunity' was strikingly close in all social classes.

In Middlesbrough working-class children lost the 'protection' of a substantial fee-paying group as early as 1935, and thereafter won a proportion of the large number of free and special places which steadily approached that to which their relative average level of measured intelligence entitled them. The actual contribution of the middle-class to the group of holders of free and special places was far below its expected level until the abolition of the small fee-paying group in 1945 forced them into the competition.

SOCIAL CLASS AND ENTRY TO GRAMMAR SCHOOL

We have so far been concerned with opportunity and ability in relation to free or special places before and after 1945. It remains to consider opportunity and ability in relation to *all* places, whether open to competition or not.

The actual distribution of places of all kinds at various periods is shown in Table 8 (p. 61), against the expected distribution for the same periods, which is now calculated on the basis of the total number of grammar school places annually available and not merely of the number open to competition.

Column 1 of Table 8 shows a fall in the minimum IQ required for entry to a grammar school which would follow from the increase shown in column 8 in the numbers of boys admitted annually, if the assumption were correct that the size of the age-group remained constant. But, in fact, the age-group increased in both areas. In Middlesbrough, the increase of the annual intake to the grammar schools was far greater than that of the age-group, so that the decline in the minimum IQ shown is not seriously exaggerated. In South West Hertfordshire, however, the growth of the annual intake to the grammar schools did not quite keep pace with that of the age-group. Although the catchment area of the grammar schools of the Division has narrowed, compensating to some extent for the stiffening of the competition for places, the minimum IQ may have actually remained at the pre-1918 level, or even have risen slightly rather than fallen as is shown in column 1. This would have the effect of reducing the expected intake of working-class boys shown in column 6, so that the discrepancy between the expected and actual intake of these boys (columns 6 and 7) in the years before 1945 is probably slightly exaggerated.

It is nevertheless clear that although a rough equality of opportunity was established in Middlesbrough as early as the 1920's, in South West Hertfordshire many able boys of working-class origin were excluded from the grammar schools before 1945. Indeed, it seems likely that for every able boy from a working-class family who was admitted two or three were excluded. The post-war revolution has been a reality in South West Hertfordshire, establishing the same equality of opportunity there as has existed in Middlesbrough for 25 or 30 years. In 1952 virtually the full quota of boys with the necessary minimum intellectual qualification was admitted from every social class to grammar schools.

We may compare our findings with those of J. L. Gray and P. Moshinsky[1] in their study of a representative sample of London children attending private and preparatory as well as public elementary schools in 1933-34.

They showed that there was a striking positive relationship between the social origins of able children and their chances of obtaining entry to a grammar (then 'secondary') school, or its equivalent in the independent system. Thus, while nearly all the children of the larger business owners

[1] Op cit. in Hogben, L. (ed.), op. cit.

and the professional classes who possessed high ability had
the opportunity of higher education, the corresponding
figure for clerical and commercial employees was 50 per
cent., for skilled wage earners 30 per cent. and for unskilled
wage earners 20 per cent.[1] Conversely, at a lower level of
ability, only 1 per cent. of the children of unskilled workers
had the opportunity of a higher education, compared with
nearly 50 per cent. of the children of larger business owners
and 35 per cent. of those of professional workers. Although
our data differ in important respects[2] the comparison with
earlier findings is worth making and is set out below. For
each occupational group the number of children[3] given a
grammar school education is expressed as a percentage of
the number of children with 'high ability' in that group. A
percentage of 100 for each group would indicate that able
children, whatever their origins, had free access to grammar
schools.

---

[1] p. 416-17.

[2] In South West Hertfordshire and Middlesbrough, children in
independent schools were included only if they took part in the
selection examination, and no account was taken of opportunities for
a grammar school education, or its equivalent, in schools not on the
Ministry's Grant List.

The definition of 'high ability' was also different. Gray and Moshinsky
used an IQ of 130 or more on the basis of the Otis Advanced Group
Intelligence Test (Form A), which was the level achieved by 50% of
the fee-paying pupils in the schools at that time. In South West
Hertfordshire and Middlesbrough, Moray House IQ's were used,
respectively of 112+ and 114+, being the points at which the successful
were divided from the unsuccessful in the selection examinations in
the years of our enquiry. These IQ's represent the minimum qualification for admission to a grammar school in those years. They are
slightly lower than the hypothetical minimum IQ's calculated for boys
only on p. 46 above, since in practice selection is made on the basis
of a total score which includes the results of tests in Arithmetic and
English as well as in Intelligence. At the higher level and for boys only,
the correspondence between ability and opportunity is even closer
than appears from the table above (see Table 8, p. 61).

[3] To make possible the comparison with the findings of Gray and
Moskinsky, the figures for Middlesbrough and South West Hertfordshire in this case include both boys and girls.

	London	South West Hertfordshire	Middlesbrough	
	(1933-34)	(1952)	(1953)	
Professional	153·9 ⎫			Professional
Larger business		96·4	100·0	workers and
owners	195·3 ⎬			business owners
Minor professional	103·8 ⎭			and managers
Small business				Foremen, small
owners	29·2 ⎫	101·8	113·8	shopkeepers, etc.
Shopkeepers	56·5 ⎭			
Clerical and				
commercial	68·0	83·7	113·3	Clerical workers
Skilled manual	35·1	98·2	93·2	Skilled manual
Unskilled manual	23·2	83·7	87·2	Unskilled manual

NOTE *on the Procedure of Selection for Secondary Schools, South West Hertfordshire and Middlesbrough*

The very close similarity in both areas between the numbers of children of each occupational group who were allocated to grammar schools in the years of our enquiry and the numbers who might have been expected to gain admission had places been allocated on the basis of intelligence test performance only, is the more surprising when it is recalled that the selection procedures employed were fairly complex and included several different measures of ability. It is worth scrutinizing more closely the methods used in order to obtain a clearer picture of the part played by intelligence tests (no longer in use in South West Hertfordshire) and to examine the possibility, particularly at the borderline of success, of the influence of social bias on the results of the examination from sources other than the social distribution of intelligence.

In South West Hertfordshire in 1952 an intelligence test was employed as a preliminary screen. All children who were qualified by age to take the County Entrance examination were given this test in November 1951. Head Teachers of Primary schools were thus enabled to decide which children were suitable candidates for the County Entrance examination. No guidance was given to Heads either as to the numbers which they should send forward or as to what should be regarded as a minimum test score. A Head Teacher could, if he wished, enter all his pupils or none at all, although parents had the right to request that a child be presented for examination despite advice to the contrary. The second part of the examination took place in March 1952 and consisted of standardized papers in English and Arithmetic, a second Intelligence Test and a General Paper. The General Paper was used only to provide subsidiary information in deciding the fate of borderline cases. From the other papers a composite score was obtained, made up of the average of the Intelligence test scores, plus the English and the Arithmetic scores. The candidates were thus listed in order of performance and divided into three groups. Those in the highest group were offered grammar school places after a formal interview by a Board consisting of the grammar school Heads and the Head Teacher of a primary school in another part of the County. The remaining grammar school places were filled from the intermediate group ('the pool'). The candidates in this group were interviewed by the same Board, which took the General Paper into account in reaching its decision.

The selection procedure in Middlesbrough in 1953 differed from that of Hertfordshire in that no preliminary test was carried out. In March 1953 all children in the appropriate age-group took an Intelligence test and standardized English and Arithmetic tests. The results of the three tests were used, as in Hertfordshire, to compile a composite score, although the separate test scores were scrutinized and minimum scores in the separate tests were required as a condition of a place in the grammar schools. In addition, to aid the assessment of borderline candidates, a Composition test was administered, and the schools were asked to give, as percentage marks, teachers' estimates of capacity in English and Arithmetic. Special consideration was given to cases where there was a discrepancy between Head Teachers' recommendations and test results, and the results of an Intelligence test taken by all candidates twelve months before the examination were also taken into account where appropriate. The estimates for each school were scaled against the IQ's obtained in that school, thus giving scaled estimates in a form which not only enabled them to be compared with the scores obtained in the Moray House tests, but also enabled one school to be compared with another. Less use was made of the interview than in South West Hertfordshire; about nine-tenths of the grammar school places available were offered on the basis of examination performance and teachers' estimates only. The remaining vacancies were awarded to 'borderline' candidates after the interviewers' judgments and other relevant educational information had been considered. In South West Hertfordshire about two-thirds of the grammar school places had been filled from the 'recommended lists', but even these successful pupils were formally interviewed.

Theoretically it is possible that the inclusion in the selection procedure of two types of process over and above intelligence test performance might affect the educational destiny of children of different social origins in two ways. Biased subjective judgment is one of these, and diversity of performance in English and Arithmetic at a given level of intelligence is the other.

In South West Hertfordshire, in particular, subjective judgment entered into the selection procedure at two important stages. In the first place, only those children whose chances of success seemed reasonable to their Head Teachers, or whose parents insisted upon their right to be considered, took the whole of the County Entrance examination. It seemed worth while to examine the possibility that in making their decisions Head Teachers were guided to some extent by more or less stereotyped conceptions of what constituted 'good grammar school material'—conceptions which might have the effect of reducing the chances of children from families low in the occupational scale.

It is true that the proportion of children recommended

by the Heads of primary schools for entry to the complete
examination varied considerably and consistently down the
occupational scale, the proportion from the highest group
being twice as great as that from the lowest. If, however,
there had been any conscious or unconscious bias at work,
we should expect to find it reflected in the examination performance of the children who passed through the preliminary test. If these varying proportions reflect the application
of more stringent standards to children of working-class
families, their examination results would, if anything, be
superior to those of the middle-class children whose social
advantages had presumably compensated, in the judgment
of Head Teachers, for intellectual inferiority. Our analysis
gave no indication of any such bias. Indeed, although
almost all the middle-class children took the complete
examination, as compared with about one half of the
children of manual workers, the performance of the latter
group was on the average somewhat inferior. This was true
both of their results in the preliminary tests of intelligence
and of their performance in the whole of the subsequent
examination. It seems that in doubtful cases the standards
applied by Head Teachers to working-class children were, if
anything, more rather than less generous.

The interviewing of the 'pool' candidates is the second
point at which the influence of subjective factors might be
expected. It seems, however, that even within this comparatively narrow intellectual range the relationship between
examination performance and the judgment of the interviewing Board was so close as virtually to outweigh the
influence of any other element. This was ascertained by
dividing the 'pool' candidates into three categories, each
representing a range of about ten points in total score, and
examining the success rates of the various occupational
groups within each category.

In the case of the intermediate group there is some hint
of a consistent relationship between social origins and the
results of the interview. However, the number of middle-

class children in this category was extremely small, and no great weight could be attached to these variations in success rates which were not accompanied by any comparable trend in either the upper or the lower category of 'pool' candidates.

It seems clear that in South West Hertfordshire the working-class child is not handicapped in competing for grammar school places by open or implicit bias on the part of Head Teachers. One other factor needs to be considered, and in this case account can be taken of the position in both areas. It is sometimes suggested—and there is some evidence in support of the theory—that when IQ is held constant there is a correlation between socio-economic status and performance in attainment tests. This is based on the assumption that English and Arithmetic tests reflect social and cultural influences to a greater extent than do intelligence tests. The extent to which such factors may have been at work in our sample was assessed by considering the children falling within successive narrow ranges of measured intelligence at the borderline of selection, and ascertaining whether, at given levels of intelligence, there were any significant differences between the mean attainment test scores of occupational groups. Mean scores in English and Arithmetic tests were calculated for children whose Intelligence Quotient fell between 105 and 109, 110 and 114, and 115 and 119 respectively. It was quite clear that at each IQ level the differences between means were slight and statistically insignificant, and that they bore no systematic relationship to occupational class. For example, in two of the IQ groups in South West Hertfordshire the mean English quotient of the middle-class children was slightly higher than that of the children of skilled manual workers, while in the third group their mean score was slightly lower. On the other hand, the mean Arithmetic quotient of the children of skilled manual workers was higher at each level of intelligence than that of the middle-class children, though not significantly higher.

It seemed justifiable to conclude, therefore, that neither

subjective bias nor diversity of performance in attainment tests, relative to intelligence, is in fact prejudicing the chances of working-class children. The present differences in proportion of the contribution of the various occupational classes to the grammar school intake can be explained almost entirely in terms of the unequal distribution of measured intelligence.

Table 6

SOCIAL DISTRIBUTION OF MEASURED INTELLIGENCE AMONG ENTRANTS TO SECONDARY SCHOOLS

SOUTH WEST HERTFORDSHIRE (1952)

Father's Occupation	No. of children	Mean IQ	Standard Deviation
Professional workers, business owners and managers	98	112·95	11·62
Clerical workers	104	109·15	12·59
Foremen, small shopkeepers, etc.	243	103·70	13·47
Skilled manual workers	583	100·10	12·79
Unskilled manual workers	288	97·15	13·24
Total	1,316	100·97	14·15

MIDDLESBROUGH (1953)

Father's Occupation	CATHOLIC CHILDREN			OTHERS		
	No.	Mean IQ	Standard Deviation	No.	Mean IQ	Standard Deviation
Professional workers, business owners, and managers	11	121·37	8·52	42	115·24	12·0
Clerical workers	(1)	—	—	42	108·23	12·97
Foremen, small shopkeepers, etc.	24	102·92	15·75	98	104·36	13·06
Skilled manual workers	72	98·51	16·63	306	99·05	13·24
Unskilled manual workers	86	98·72	15·09	267	96·50	12·94
Total	194*	100·49	16·41	755*	100·43	14·09

* These numbers represent a 50% sample of the age-group.

Table 7

EXPECTED AND ACTUAL SOCIAL DISTRIBUTION OF *FREE AND SPECIAL* PLACES FOR BOYS IN GRAMMAR SCHOOLS AT VARIOUS PERIODS

Period	Hypothetical Minimum IQ	Middle-Class Expected	Middle-Class Actual	Lower Middle-Class Expected	Lower Middle-Class Actual	Working-Class Expected	Working-Class Actual	Annual intake of free or special place holders
	1	2 %	3 %	4 %	5 %	6 %	7 %	8 (N)
A. SOUTH WEST HERTFORDSHIRE								
1904-18	129·5	21	13	50	43	29	44	24
1922-30	127·5	24	4	49	40	27	56	33
1934-38	126·5	24	2	46	50	28	48	37
1943	125·0	23	6	47	44	30	50	43
1945	116·7	16	31	40	44	44	25	113
1952	114·2	15	15	37	34	48	51	145
B. MIDDLESBROUGH								
1905-18	129·5	5	12	55	35	40	53	20
1922-30	126·8	15	8	45	27	40	65	40
1935-38	118·5	24	12	28	32	48	56	111
1939-44	117·5	24	11	29	32	47	52	119
1945	116·5	23	14	28	34	49	52	130
1948-51	115·5	21	15	29	31	50	54	139
1953	114·8	24	23	29	32	47	45	148

Table 8

EXPECTED AND ACTUAL SOCIAL DISTRIBUTION OF PLACES FOR BOYS IN GRAMMAR SCHOOLS AT VARIOUS PERIODS

Period	Hypothetical Minimum IQ (1)	Middle-Class Expected (2) %	Middle-Class Actual (3) %	Lower Middle-Class Expected (4) %	Lower Middle-Class Actual (5) %	Working-Class Expected (6) %	Working-Class Actual (7) %	Annual intake of boys (N) (8)
A. SOUTH WEST HERTFORDSHIRE								
1904-18	117·8	18	31	40	54	42	15	97
1922-30	116·4	15	28	39	52	46	20	116
1934-38	115·9	16	19	38	64	47	17	122
1943	115·6	15	24	38	50	47	26	126
1945	116·7	16	31	40	44	44	25	113
1952	114·2	15	15	37	34	48	51	145
B. MIDDLESBROUGH								
1905-18	125·3	4	31	56	46	40	23	52
1922-30	121·5	15	23	45	39	40	38	88
1935-38	115·8	24	17	28	36	48	47	137
1939-44	114·8	24	14	29	34	47	52	148
1945	116·5	23	14	28	34	49	52	130
1948-51	115·5	21	15	29	31	50	54	139
1953	114·8	24	23	29	32	47	45	148

PART III

ENVIRONMENT AND OPPORTUNITY

UNDER the present procedure of selection and the provision of places being what it is, the opportunity for children of working-class origin to receive secondary grammar school education is limited by their lower average measured intelligence; the limit of their opportunity had been reached in the years of our enquiry in Middlesbrough and South West Hertfordshire. The social distribution of successful candidates in the selection tests has been shown to be closely related to the social distribution of measured intelligence. But this does not dispose of the problem of equality of educational opportunity. Measured intelligence is well known to be largely an acquired characteristic.[1] Though we may legitimately infer an important genetic component, we cannot observe or measure it and we are under an obligation to examine the differences of environment which undoubtedly contribute largely to differences in measured intelligence, even though they cannot be held wholly responsible for them.

It is not our intention, however, to enter into the complex and controversial question of the relative weight which should be attached to hereditary and environmental factors in the intelligence test scores of children at the age of 11. We cannot do more than make a fresh attempt to throw light on the influence which certain elements of a child's environment have on his chances of selection for a grammar school. Indirectly, of course, this means a study of the impact of these environmental factors on his intelligence test score, since this is frequently an important item in the total score on the basis of which the selection is made, and is

---

[1] See Vernon, P. E., in *The Bearings of Recent Advances in Psychology on Educational Problems* (1955) for an authoritative restatement of the issue.

in any case closely correlated with success in the examination. But although measured intelligence underlies all the differences we shall be investigating—part symptom, part cause—we shall put it to one side in the discussion which follows, and seek instead the answers to two more straightforward questions: firstly, in what respects do the family and primary school environments of successful and unsuccessful candidates differ at each social level? and secondly, how are particular features, separately considered, of home and school environment related to success in the selection examination?

The favourable attitudes of their parents to their education might reasonably be expected to stand out as a distinguishing feature of the home environment of children who are successful in the selection examination. The part played by the material environment of the home is more difficult to assess. How far do favourable attitudes and educational aspirations on the part of parents compensate for the handicap of an otherwise poor home? At what point does the material environment of the home nullify parental attitudes and ambitions? On the other hand, can a splendid new primary school improve the prospects of success of children whose homes are materially poor, or whose parents are not in sympathy with its educational tasks?

It is easy to see that a child's environment must exercise a considerable influence on his chances of selection, and that there are wide differences in home and school environment underlying and reinforcing the social distribution of measured intelligence which the distribution of places in grammar schools today reflects; but it is much more difficult to disentangle from the complex of mutually determining and reinforcing influences, limitations, incentives and opportunities of which the environment is composed, any series of outstanding features to which independent weight can be given. No great claims can be made for the following analysis, or for the material on which it is based; the latter does not allow of refined statistical analysis. We hope to be in a better position to discuss these complex issues at the end of the second stage of our enquiries. It seemed to us, however, that it would be useful as a first approach to the problem, to relate the comparatively narrow range of differences in the home and school environment of children drawn from families at the same social level, to variations in their chances of success in the selection examination. In other words, we would examine the problem of environmental differences and their relation to success at eleven plus, with the factor of social class held constant. Moreover, the differences *within* social classes are assuming a new importance now that we have a Welfare State and, within the limits of the existing organization of education, a formal equality of opportunity.

It is intended, therefore, in the following chapters to compare the economic circumstances and living conditions of our sample of families in each area, divided into occupational groups and broader social classes. The material conditions under which boys and girls from these families were educated up to the age of 10, and the attitudes and preferences of their parents regarding their education and future prospects will also be examined. We shall be concerned not merely with the marked difference *between* the social classes in the material environment of homes and in the attitudes and preferences of parents in educational matters, but with these differences of environment *within* social classes, relating them to the children's success in the selection tests for secondary education, and attempting an assessment of their relative importance for the children's chances of success.

CHAPTER 5

FAMILY AND PRIMARY SCHOOL ENVIRONMENT OF ENTRANTS TO SECONDARY SCHOOLS

SOURCES OF INFORMATION

Two sources of information were available concerning the environment of children in relation to their chances of selection for secondary education: interviews in their homes with the parents of children about to enter secondary schools, and enquiries into the material environment of the primary schools attended by these children. In both areas the interviews with parents took place either just before or soon after the entrance examination and in all cases before the results were announced. The object was to obtain information concerning the occupations and education of the parents and to discover something about the child's home environment under two broad heads—*material environment* (i.e. basic income, size of family, type of house and available space per person) and *'cultural' environment* (i.e. the 'family atmosphere', in so far as this could be assessed as likely to be favourable or unfavourable to the progress of the child's education).

To discover the material environment of the home the following questions[1] were asked: the father's occupation; the present and pre-marital occupation of the mother; the

---

[1] The survey in South West Hertfordshire was preceded by a small pilot enquiry, on the basis of which some questions were omitted and others reformulated, and some additional questions were introduced. The interviews were carried out by undergraduate and post-graduate students in March and April 1952 in South West Hertfordshire, and twelve months later in Middlesbrough. The investigators were well received by parents. In South West Hertfordshire, the names and

age and education of both parents; their length of residence in the district; the size of the household; the number of children and the ordinal position in the family of the child under consideration; the net income of the head of the household; the type of house and the number of rooms, and whether the family possessed a motor car, a telephone or television set. To assess the favourable or unfavourable atmosphere of the home the parent was asked to give his estimate of the importance of the move to the secondary school; his knowledge of the selection procedure; the number of his visits to the school during the past year and the reasons for them; whether he had met the child's present Class Teacher or Head Teacher, and if so whether he had ever discussed the child's secondary education with either of them; whether he belonged to a Parent/Teacher Association; which type of secondary school he preferred for his child and the reasons for his preference; the strength of his preference for the grammar school, if this was his choice; his readiness to accept for his child a place in a grammar school, should one be offered, if he had expressed no such preference in the first place; the age up to which he hoped his child would attend school and his preferences in the matter of further education; the type of work which he would prefer his child to take up, and the reasons for his choice; the daily and Sunday newspapers and magazines he

---

addresses were obtained of the 1,575 children who took the preliminary intelligence test either from public primary or private schools. The parents of 1,457 (92·5 per cent.) were interviewed. The balance included cases in which co-operation was refused; cases in which, despite repeated calls, neither parent could be traced; and cases in which the child was known to be in the care of the local authority.

In Middlesbrough, we attempted to interview the parents of only 50 per cent. of the children in the relevant age group, stratified by schools. These amounted to 1,081 (including known orphans) and 1,037 interviews were carried out. The final response rate (95·8 per cent.) was higher than in Hertfordshire, as in those cases where no contact was made with the parent the name of a substitute child was drawn at random from the list of pupils not included in the 50 per cent. sample. No attempt was made to draw substitutes in cases of refusal.

See the Note on the Statistical Reliability of Tables, p. 152.

read; whether he belonged to the public library and to any local organizations; his religious affiliation.

The primary schools attended by these children (though not the 'private' schools outside the public system) were visited and an assessment was made of the material environment in thich whey had been taught before the selection tests. No attempt was made to study the influence of social factors of a more subtle kind on the primary school experience of the children. However, a correlation between the success of primary schools in obtaining grammar school places and the material environment in which they have to work has been frequently indicated. It was felt worth while to include a study of this factor since by using information about children's schools as well as about their homes, it was possible to go somewhat further than previous investigators in isolating the influence of particular factors of environment on children's chances of success in the selection tests. A number of indices were devised to facilitate the study of this problem.

An *'index of material environment'* took into account the nature of the school structure itself—its age, the extent of the teaching, dining and sanitary accommodation, and the size of the playground and of any additional playing space. Primary school buildings in both areas were graded on a five-point scale ranging from those which conformed with modern standards of lay-out and amenities (category 5) to those which were completely out of date and incapable of satisfactory alteration (Category 1).[1] Thus:

---

[1] An assessment of standards of school environment was included in the survey of Middlesbrough reported by Ruth Glass, op. cit., p. 110. Similar principles and the same five categories of assessment were used to compile the *Index of Material Environment* for the present study; but the exact formula of the earlier Middlesbrough survey was not adhered to. The rating was intended to be one of 'bricks and mortar' and physical layout rather than of the use made of the buildings or of the number or type of children. An independent assignment of each school to one of the five categories was made in South West Hertfordshire by the Building Surveyor and in Middlesbrough by the Architect to the Education Department; in almost every case the assignments were identical and discrepancies were eliminated by discussion.

Category 5: built in accordance with modern standards, for the most part since the war; open sites; light, airy and colourful buildings; well provided with assembly halls, special purpose-, dining- and staff-rooms.

Category 4: built in the inter-war years, frequently on less open sites; usually single-storey; good windows; an assembly hall in every case, and reasonable provision for special purpose- and other rooms.

Category 3: built between 1900 and 1914, often with later modifications; sound but unimaginative structure; usually two and sometimes three storeys; playing space may be restricted; and the assembly hall may be a makeshift combination of classrooms.

Category 2: though sound in structure, usually more than 50 years old and therefore providing inferior accommodation by modern standards; no assembly halls, dining-, staff-, or special purpose-rooms.

Category 1: of similar age and type to category 2, but in worse condition and often inferior in siting or design.

It was important to be able to assess the extent to which children from poor homes tend also to be taught under adverse conditions at school. For this purpose the proportion of the fathers of children at each school indicated in the Electoral Register as being liable for jury service was used as an index (termed *the Juror Index*)[1] of the socio-economic level of the population served by the school.

MATERIAL CONDITIONS AT HOME

The children in our samples in Middlesbrough and South West Hertfordshire are reared under very varied conditions at home and have been taught in primary schools of very

---

[1] A property qualification renders residents liable for jury service. The proportion of the population with this qualification gives a measure of the socio-economic status of a district, which has been shown to be reasonably reliable. (See P. G. Gray, T. Corlett, and P. Jones: The Proportion of Jurors as an Index of the Economic Status of a District (Social Survey, 1952).

diverse material standards. It is worth examining these regional differences before attempting to disentangle particular elements of the environment and to assess the relative strength of their influence on the educational chances of the children.

Size of Family

As might be expected, families in South West Hertfordshire tend to be smaller than in Middlesbrough, where the larger working-class population also contains a sizeable Catholic minority. In South West Hertfordshire 47 per cent. of the sample of children came from families having one or two children only. In the Middlesbrough sample 41 per cent. of the non-Catholic and 52 per cent. of the Catholic children come from families of four or more.

Distribution of Incomes[1]

The general level of incomes in South West Hertfordshire was higher than for the Middlesbrough sample. Thus, in only one-third of the families of children in our sample in South West Hertfordshire was the net income of the chief wage earner below £7 10s. per week, and in one family in four his net weekly income was above £10. In Middlesbrough, on the other hand, 38 per cent. earned less than £7 10s. per week and only in one family in six was the weekly income of the chief wager earner above £10. The unskilled manual workers in Middlesbrough appeared to be better off than their fellows in South West Hertfordshire; a greater proportion of their number received more than £7 10s. per week. But skilled workers and non-manual workers at all levels from supervisory to managerial or professional status were apparently somewhat worse off in Middlesbrough.

---

[1] 90 per cent. of the parents interviewed in both areas were willing to say within which of the following ranges their net income fell; below £7 10s. per week, £7 10s.-£10, £10 per week and over.

Housing Conditions

Some 68 per cent. of the families in South West Hertfordshire lived in detached or semi-detached houses, and 88 per cent. occupied at least enough space to provide one room per person. In Middlesbrough, however, 73 per cent. lived in terraced houses, and only 23 per cent. in detached or semi-detached houses. Only 62 per cent., a much smaller proportion than in South West Hertfordshire, occupied enough space to provide one room or more per person. In fact, the greatly inferior character of the housing available at almost any income level is an invariable feature of family environment in Middlesbrough.

MATERIAL CONDITIONS AT SCHOOL

There are substantial differences between the areas in the material standards of primary schools. A high proportion (29 per cent.) of children in Middlesbrough were still in 1953 attending unreorganized schools, and generally these were voluntary schools in poor buildings. In South West Hertfordshire in 1952 nine primary schools, accommodating some 37 per cent. of the primary population, fell into Category 5, representing the highest material standards; but in Middlesbrough only one such school came within the scope of our enquiry.[1] Eight Middlesbrough schools fell into the next highest Category 4, accommodating 30 per cent. of the children, but this did not outweigh the numbers in the new schools in South West Hertfordshire:

Material Environment Category 4 and 5	% Primary School Pupils	
	S.W. Hertfordshire	Middlesbrough
	45·2	33·7

Nine Middlesbrough schools fell into the lowest Category 1, and accommodated as many as 21 per cent. of the children; in South West Hertfordshire, schools in this category accommodated only 9·6 per cent. of the primary

---

[1] Another was in use but its pupils were all under the age of 11 at the time of the enquiry.

pupils. But taking the two lowest categories of school together the proportion in each area was much the same:

Material Environment *Category* 1 and 2	*% Primary School Pupils* *S. W. Hertfordshire* 40·2	*Middlesbrough* 41·6

Thus, the proportion of 'superior' and 'inferior' schools was roughly the same in each area, but it must be remembered that the 'superior' schools in South West Hertfordshire are often of very high standard and the 'inferior' schools in Middlesbrough of very low standard. In South West Hertfordshire three of the four schools in Category 1— the oldest and most unsatisfactory—served more or less rural districts outside the borough of Watford. In Middlesbrough the nine schools in this category were situated in congested slums. The playgrounds were small and playing fields were some distance away. In South West Hertfordshire they had open country, but, as in one case, could lack running water, storage and cloakroom space; they might have no assembly hall, and four classes could meet in three classrooms lit by gas only.

THE ASSOCIATION OF CONDITIONS AT HOME AND AT SCHOOL

In Middlesbrough the relationship between the primary school environment and the socio-economic status of the school population was much closer than in South West Hertfordshire. Schools in the densely populated more northerly districts of the town, in which the heavy industry, railways and docks are located, serve populations ranking lowest in status as measured by the Juror Index,[1] and have the oldest and least adequate (though not necessarily the most overcrowded) school buildings. Southwards, the social composition of the population 'improves'; its density decreases steadily and the school buildings are correspondingly of more recent construction and greater adequacy.

---

[1] See page 71 above.

The material environment of the primary schools continues on the whole to reinforce rather than to mitigate the influence of the material environment of the children's homes.

In South West Hertfordshire before 1942 the traditional relationship between poor schools and poor homes existed both within the Borough of Watford and in the poorer rural areas served mainly by out-of-date church schools. The new schools built to meet the needs of working class families on the Oxhey Estate have modified this relationship, but within the Borough of Watford it still holds, since one of two new schools was built to serve a middle-class residential area in the south and west of the town.

ATTITUDES AND PREFERENCES OF PARENTS[1]

The attitudes and preferences of parents regarding the secondary and further education of their children differed less in the two areas than the material environment of families and primary schools. Such differences as were revealed were what might have been expected in view of the economic circumstances and general living conditions of the population and of the variations in the distribution of further education amongst parents in our samples.[2]

Asked whether they had given much thought recently to their children's secondary education, 53 per cent. of parents in South West Hertfordshire, as against 43 per cent. of parents in Middlesbrough, declared that they had thought about the matter 'a lot'. Some 46 per cent. of Hertfordshire parents, as against 40 per cent. in Middlesbrough, stated that they had discussed the problem with someone—either the Head Teacher or the class Teacher or both—in the primary school attended by their child.

---

[1] See Martin, F. M., *An Enquiry into Parents' Preferences in Secondary Education*, in Glass, D. V. (ed.), op. cit., for a fuller analysis of the information concerning South West Hertfordshire.

[2] In South West Hertfordshire, more of the working class fathers had received some full or part time further education, but there were fewer of the clerical workers, professional and business men than in Middlesbrough, who claimed having had any sort of further education.

However, in both areas half the parents expressed the opinion that the transfer to a secondary school was an important stage in their child's career and would make a substantial difference to his future; and there was the same widespread desire for a grammar school type of secondary education. More than half the parents in both areas (54 per cent. in Middlesbrough and 56 per cent. in South West Hertfordshire) favoured the grammar school, and a further 19 per cent. decided on alternative forms of selective secondary education. In South West Hertfordshire there was also a minority (2 per cent.), which did not reveal itself in Middlesbrough, who wished their children to remain outside the public system of schools altogether.[1]

In South West Hertfordshire 15 per cent. of the parents expressly preferred the modern school, as against only 6 per cent. in Middlesbrough where the proportion of parents who felt unable, or were unwilling, to express any preference at all was relatively high (23 per cent.). It is not easy to interpret the meaning of this difference between the areas. It may be, though on the evidence it is not certain, that in South West Hertfordshire the modern schools have established themselves amongst at least a minority of parents as offering an intrinsically desirable type of secondary education.

In the matter of the school leaving age, the distribution of parents' preferences in both areas followed the general pattern of their preferences in the other matters touched on in our enquiry concerning their children's education. Thus, the proportion of parents in South West Hertfordshire favouring a leaving age of 17 or 18 (34 per cent.) was larger than in Middlesbrough (27 per cent.), whilst the proportion content with a leaving age of 15 was smaller (33 per cent. as compared with 40 per cent. in Middlesbrough).

All in all, however, despite considerable differences in

---

[1] This minority was concentrated mainly in the professional and business groups, some 10 per cent. of which shared this view.

their conditions of life, the attitudes and preferences of parents in regard to their children's secondary education differed surprisingly little in the two areas. There was, for obvious reasons, a somewhat larger element of indifference or ignorance in Middlesbrough. But amongst those—the majority in both areas—who were neither ignorant nor indifferent the national stereotype prevailed; concern with the secondary education of one's children meant in effect a preference that they should enter a grammar school, or its equivalent outside the public system.

Not only was the proportion of parents in general who expressed either a preference or a strong preference for a grammar school virtually the same in both areas, but they were also similarly distributed among the various occupational groups. (Table 9, p. 82.) A smaller proportion of parents at the bottom than at the top of the occupational scale preferred a grammar school, but in no occupational group in either area did fewer than 43 per cent. do so. The proportions in each group who were prepared to say that their preference for a grammar school was 'strong' were naturally smaller—but it might perhaps have been expected that in the lower'middle-class groups of clerical, supervisory workers, small shopkeepers, etc., the proportions (varying from 41 to 48 per cent.) with a 'strong' preference for a grammar school would have been larger, and closer to those in the professional and business group (65-75 per cent.).

'Parity of Esteem' is a myth. Yet preference for the grammar school bears no relation to the realities of the outcome of the process of selection. Some idea of the extent of parental frustration on this account may be obtained from Table 10 (p. 83), which sets out the distribution of parents whose children were allocated to other types of secondary schools despite their expressed preference for a grammar school. Parents who were prepared to describe their preference for a grammar school as 'strong' may be held to be more frustrated when their children are allocated elsewhere than those who merely declared a simple 'preference' for this type of school, and who, it may be argued, are following a convention without strong feelings in the matter. The table accordingly distinguishes between the 'mildly' and the 'strongly' frustrated.

The proportion of both 'mildly' and 'strongly' frustrated parents is naturally greatest at the bottom of the occupational scale, where the rate of success in the selection examination is lowest. The strength of the frustrated group amongst parents generally is of more interest, and it is noticeable that 'mild' and 'strong' frustration is prevalent to much the same extent in both areas: 37 per cent. of parents in South West Hertfordshire and 41 per cent. in Middlesbrough may be described as 'mildly' frustrated, and 21 and 20 per cent. respectively as 'strongly' frustrated.

The extent of parental frustration in the various occupational groups does not show such wide variation as might have been expected. The size of the 'mildly' frustrated group, taking both areas into account, ranges from 35 to 45 per cent., and that of the 'strongly' frustrated group from 16 to 27 per cent. among the occupational groups. We can perhaps legitimately ignore the 'frustration' of the professional and business parents who can in many, if not in most cases, realize their preferences by sending their children to independent schools. Among the remaining occupational groups, those in the lower middle-class show the largest minorities of frustrated parents. This is not surprising when we remember the ousting of lower middle-class children from the grammar schools, particularly since 1945 in South West Hertfordshire. Yet the frustrated minorities of skilled and unskilled working-class parents are not proportionally so very much smaller and in absolute numbers they are, of course, much larger. The differences are somewhat greater in the case of the 'strongly' than in that of the 'mildly' frustrated.

The public view still lags behind the official view as to the desirable length of the grammar school course, as Table 11 (p. 89) makes clear. Of the parents who desired a grammar school education for their children, as many as 17 per cent. in South West Hertfordshire and 20 per cent. in Middlesbrough thought nevertheless that they should leave school at 15. The proportions willing that they should finish the minimum course and leave at 16 were 32 and 35 per cent. respectively. The seven-year course, which the Hertfordshire authority informs the parents of grammar school entrants should be regarded as 'normal' for pupils in these schools, is contemplated by only 39 per cent. of the parents in the South West division of the area who would like their children to attend grammar schools, and by 31 per cent. in Middlesbrough.[1] But these figures conceal something like a post-war revolution in the views of working-class parents.

Of the surprisingly strong minorities of working-class parents in the two areas who wished their children to attend grammar schools[2] a remarkably high proportion contemplated keeping them at school at least until the end of the grammar school course; three-quarters in South West Hertfordshire and two-thirds in Middlesbrough of those choosing a grammar school also chose a leaving age of at least 16. In Middlesbrough almost one quarter and in South West Hertfordshire almost one-third of these working-class parents were prepared to contemplate the full seven-year course, i.e. a leaving age of 18 or over.[3]

The figures can, of course, be given a less favourable emphasis. There were nearly one-third (31 per cent.) of working-class parents in Middlesbrough and nearly one-quarter (23 per cent.) in South West Hertfordshire who were unwilling to look beyond the age of compulsory school attendance despite their preference for a grammar school education for their children. However, if we examine the views on this matter of those parents whose children were

---

[1] The figures for the parents of children actually selected for grammar schools are larger—53% and 44% respectively (cf. Table 12, p. 85).

[2] Some 50% in Middlesbrough and 46% in South West Hertfordshire. (cf. Table 9, p. 82).

[3] cf. Table 11 (p. 84).

actually selected for admission to grammar schools, we find that the problem is a smaller one (Table 12, p. 85). Thus, only one-fifth of working-class parents of children allocated to grammar schools, in the year of our enquiry in Middlesbrough, and as few as 13 per cent. in South West Hertfordshire, had previously stated their preference for a leaving age of 15 or less.[1]

It must be admitted, of course, that small proportions may represent substantial absolute numbers of children, and that the latter are the true measure of the problem for the grammar schools. In fact, the schools may find that one in seven (in Middlesbrough) and one in twelve (South West Hertfordshire) of the children admitted each year (regardless of social origin) are handicapped by the likelihood that his parents will withdraw him at the age of 15 and the certainty that they will not resist any inclination on his part to leave school at this age. They may also have to face the fact that approximately another one in four in South West Hertfordshire and one in three in Middlesbrough will be in the same position at the age of 16.

The further education of their children on leaving school was also discussed with parents during the interview.[2] The differences in the views of parents of the two areas were very small and very much as expected. The views of middle and lower middle-class parents were virtually identical in both areas; some 40 per cent. desired a university or equivalent academic course of further education for their children, and a further 19 per cent. preferred other courses of a non-academic kind, whilst approximately one-third were undecided ('don't know' or 'it depends'), leaving

---

[1] In the event, the proportion of children from working-class families who fail to complete the grammar school course in these areas may be even lower than these figures suggest. Thus, in Middlesbrough, of the sons of manual workers leaving the grammar schools between 1948 and 1950, only some 15% had not completed the course at 16.

[2] The figures quoted in the text below which are not taken from Table 13 may, nevertheless, be derived from it.

only 7 per cent. who definitely wished their children to have no further education of any kind. Working-class parents in both areas were divided in similar proportions between those desiring some form of further education for their children (45 per cent.) and those who were uncertain or definitely preferred none (54 per cent.). But Middlesbrough parents in the former group preferred 'non-academic' courses more frequently than those in South West Hertfordshire, and there were more among the Middlesbrough parents in the latter group who were ready to declare that they desired no further education for their children. In both areas, of the parents who wished their children to attend grammar schools, some 30 to 40 per cent. of the middle-class, and over 50 per cent. of the working-class, either desired no further education for their children or were uncertain in the matter (Table 13, p. 86). Among the middle-class parents of both areas there was a group of much the same size (40 per cent.) who were uncertain of their attitude to any further education, and yet contemplated allowing their children to stay on at school to the age of 17 or 18. Amongst working-class parents this group was in evidence but, as might be expected, was considerably smaller (21 per cent. in South West Hertfordshire and 26 per cent. in Middlesbrough).

Local conditions do not appear to have any marked effect upon the distribution and consistency of the views of parents of children aged 10-11 as to the importance of secondary education, particularly in grammar schools, the age to which they contemplate keeping their children at school, and the desirability of further education. Although relatively few parents have no original intention of allowing their children to complete the grammar school course, there is much more doubt in all strata of the population as to the desirability of further education, even amongst those who contemplate the full seven-year secondary course for their children.

Table 9

SOCIAL CLASS AND PREFERENCE FOR GRAMMAR SCHOOL

	No. of Parents	Percentage preferring Grammar School	Percentage with 'strong' preference for Grammar School
SOUTH WEST HERTFORDSHIRE (1952)			
Professional and business	104	82	65
Clerical	107	77	49
Foremen, etc.	256	61	43
Skilled workers	632	48	28
Unskilled workers	313	43	20
Total	1412	54	34
MIDDLESBROUGH (1953)			
Professional and business	52	87	75
Clerical	46	67	41
Foremen, etc.	137	68	43
Skilled workers	398	53	29
Unskilled workers	378	48	22
Total	1011*	56	31

* This figure represents a 50% sample of the parents of the age-group.

Table 10

'FRUSTRATED PARENTS'*

	Parents preferring strong Grammar School whose children were sent elsewhere	Parents with strong preference for Grammar School whose children were sent elsewhere	Frustrated Parents as percentage of all parents	
			'Mildly' Frustrated	'Strongly' Frustrated
SOUTH WEST HERTFORD-SHIRE				
Professional and	%	%	%	%
business	49	47	40	31
Clerical	59	48	45	23
Foremen, etc.	70	64	42	27
Skilled workers ..	72	67	35	19
Unskilled workers ..	79	78	34	16
Total	69	63	37	21
MIDDLESBROUGH				
Professional and	%	%	%	%
business	27	23	23	17
Clerical	55	58	37	24
Foremen, etc.	68	57	46	24
Skilled workers ..	80	74	42	21
Unskilled workers ..	84	76	41	17
Total	73	64	41	20

* See pp. 77-8 above.

Table 11

PARENTS' PREFERENCES: SCHOOL LEAVING AGE IN RELATION TO CHOICE OF SECONDARY SCHOOL

Type of Secondary School preferred

Leaving Age preferred	Grammar		Central or Technical		Modern or No Preference	
	Working-Class %	Other %	Working-Class %	Other %	Working-Class %	Other %
SOUTH WEST HERTFORDSHIRE (1952)						
15 years	23	10	39	38	70	50
16 ,,	37	26	40	41	19	35
17 ,,	8	14	7	6	1	3
18+,,	32	49	12	14	7	12
No preference	0	1	2	1	3	0
Total	100	100	100	100	100	100
(N)	(440)	(323)	(206)	(64)	(290)	(58)
MIDDLESBROUGH (1953)						
15 years	31	14	46	19	69	39
16 ,,	36	32	37	59	18	31
17 ,,	8	6	6	6	2	8
18+,,	24	47	10	16	9	19
No preference	1	1	1	0	2	3
Total	100	100	100	100	100	100
(N)*	(373)	(165)	(148)	(32)	(253)	(36)

* These numbers are based on a 50% sample of the age-group.

Table 12

SCHOOL LEAVING AGE PREFERRED BY PARENTS OF CHILDREN
AWARDED GRAMMAR SCHOOL PLACES

	% preferring leaving age of				
	15	16	17	18+	No preference
SOUTH WEST HERTFORDSHIRE (1952)					
Middle Class	0	8	13	79	0
Lower Middle Class	6	31	12	51	0
Working Class	13	34	6	44	3
All	8	28	10	53	1
MIDDLESBROUGH (1953)					
Middle Class	0	24	3	73	0
Lower Middle Class	14	36	4	44	2
Working Class	20	38	8	33	1
All	14	35	6	44	1

Note: The numbers on which the percentages are based may be found in Table 14, p. 100 below.

Table 13

PARENTS' PREFERENCES: FURTHER EDUCATION IN RELATION TO CHOICE OF SECONDARY SCHOOL

Further Education preferred	Type of Secondary School preferred					
	Grammar		Central or Technical		Modern or No Preference	
	Working-Class %	Other %	Working-Class %	Other %	Working-Class %	Other %
SOUTH WEST HERTFORDSHIRE (1952)						
University or equivalent Academic Courses	29	47	20	25	11	12
Non-Academic Courses	21	16	33	29	24	26
No further education	6	6	15	10	21	12
'Don't Know' or 'It Depends'	44	31	32	36	44	50
Total	100	100	100	100	100	100
(N)	(437)	(320)	(202)	(63)	(290)	(57)
MIDDLESBROUGH (1953)						
University or equivalent Academic Courses	25	52	19	26	7	9
Non-Academic Courses	25	17	51	32	18	23
No further education	13	3	8	5	36	32
'Don't Know' or 'It Depends'	37	28	22	37	39	36
Total	100	100	100	100	100	100
(N)*	(380)	(167)	(150)	(38)	(229)	(22)

* These figures are based on a 50% sample of the age-group.

CHAPTER 6

SOCIAL FACTORS IN SELECTION FOR GRAMMAR SCHOOLS

WE HAVE seen in the last Chapter that there are surprisingly few regional differences in the nature and social distribution of parents' views as to the secondary and further education of their children; and, moreover, that what are often taken to be characteristically 'middle-class' attitudes and ambitions in the matter of education are, in fact, widespread among parents much lower in the occupational scale. We have also seen, however, that there are marked regional differences in the material conditions in which the children of these parents are being reared and educated. We turn now to consider how the material and cultural conditions of children's environment are respectively related to their chances of being selected for admission to a grammar school.

Our object in this chapter is, first, to make a general comparison of certain features of the home environment of successful and unsuccessful candidates in the 11+ examination at each social level; secondly, to examine the relationship of various features of the environment taken separately to success in the examination. We also make a closer analysis of the information concerning working-class children with the object of assessing the relative influence of various features of their environment on their chances of success in the examination.

HOME ENVIRONMENT OF SUCCESSFUL AND UNSUCCESSFUL CHILDREN[1]

Material Prosperity and Parents' Attitudes

Both in Middlesbrough and in South West Hertfordshire

---

[1] See Table 14, p. 100 below, for details of the social distribution of awards of grammar school places in the years of our enquiry in Middlesbrough and South West Hertfordshire.

and at each social level, the parents of successful children
were on the whole better educated than those of unsuccessful
children. As can be seen from Table 15 (p. 101), the percentage of fathers and mothers who had received selective
secondary schooling and some further education was nearly
twice as high amongst the successful as amongst the unsuccessful children in South West Hertfordshire, and three
times as high in Middlesbrough; and the same is true in
varying degrees at each social level. The mothers of successful working class children moreover had frequently before
marriage followed an occupation 'superior' to that of their
husbands.[1]

Not surprisingly, these better educated parents of
successful children, as indicated in Table 16 (p. 102), were
to a marked degree more interested in and ambitious for
their educational future than were the parents of unsuccessful children. They had a better knowledge of the rather
complex procedure employed in allocating children to the
different types of secondary school and had more frequently
visited the child's primary school to discuss his secondary
education with his teachers. They showed a clearer aware-
ness of the long-term importance of selective secondary
education and expressed a marked preference for the
grammar school. As compared with the parents of unsuccessful children, they favoured a longer school life,
preferred further education of the academic type for their
children (i.e. at a university rather than a technical college)
and looked forward to seeing their children enter non-
manual rather than manual occupations.

Thus, the favourable attitudes of their parents to their
education distinguished the successful from the unsuccessful

---

[1]   *Percentage of mothers whose occupation*
                                 before marriage was superior to that of the
                                 father

	Successful	Unsuccessful
South West Hertfordshire ..	39	20
Middlesbrough	12	7

children in both areas. But the part played by the material prosperity of their homes was strikingly different. As Table 17 (p. 103) shows, in South West Hertfordshire at a given social level the children who gained grammar school places were not those whose parents earned the highest incomes, nor did they enjoy superior standards of housing. In Middlesbrough, on the other hand, the successful children at each social level were distinguished by the relative material prosperity of their homes.

Now let us look at the same information about the family environment of the children in our samples from a different point of view relating the distribution of awards of grammar school places at each social level in turn to the basic income of the household, housing conditions, parents' education and interest in their children's education. In South West Hertfordshire the rates of success in the competition for places are virtually the same for all families at a given social level, whether their income is rated 'high' or 'low' or whether they occupy a detached, a semi-detached, or a terraced house. But in Middlesbrough the more prosperous families at each social level show markedly superior rates (Table 18, p, 104). Thus, for instance, of the children of skilled workers, in our Middlesbrough sample, proportionally twice as many were successful among those whose fathers earned a basic income of more than £7 10s. per week and occupied a detached or semi-detached rather than a terraced house as among those from the less prosperous and well-housed families.

There is, however, no such marked difference between the areas in the relation of success to the educational background of parents and their interest in and ambitions for their children's educational future. In both areas (Table 19, p. 105) at all social levels there was a noticeably higher proportion of awards to those children whose parents had enjoyed a selective secondary education, or some further education, and in the case of working-class children, to those whose mother's occupation before marriage was of superior standing to that of their father.[1] The importance of parents' attitudes was marked in both areas at all social levels as may be seen from Table 20, p. 106. Thus of those children of skilled workers in both areas whose parents had expressed a strong preference for a grammar school for their child's secondary education, or who had shown enough interest in their child's future to discuss it with the Head or a Class teacher at the primary school, twice as high a proportion were successful as of children at the same social level whose parents took less interest in their education.

Evidently, the general level of material prosperity *in all social classes* in South West Hertfordshire is high enough to prevent its having any consistent influence on success rates; the education, attitudes and ambitions of parents are left as the only clearly distinguishing characteristics of successful candidates and the only consistent environmental influences on the rate at which children in every social class succeed in obtaining grammar school places. These factors are also important in the case of Middlesbrough children; but the influence of the material environment of homes there cannot be discounted in the same way.

Size of Family

Size of family is a factor which in both areas is inversely related to success in the selection examination (Table 21, p. 101). It cannot be regarded simply as a feature of the material environment of homes, although it obviously has important economic implications. In the first place, it is a well-established fact that, for whatever reason, children from large families score less well on the average in intelligence tests than children from small families even at the same

---

[1]

	Percentage awarded Grammar School places of those whose mothers' occupation before marriage was	
	'Superior'	'Inferior'
South West Hertfordshire ..	24	12
Middlesbrough	18	11

social level.[1] Moreover, it is noteworthy that the inverse relationship of success to size of family was much less marked for the children of Catholic families in Middlesbrough[2] despite the fact that the fathers of some three-quarters of these large Catholic families were unskilled workers.

However that may be, we find that in South West Hertfordshire 17 per cent. of the children of unskilled workers with families of only one or two children were successful, as compared with 2 per cent. of those whose families numbered five or more. In Middlesbrough the corresponding figures for the non-Catholic unskilled workers were 9 per cent. and 3 per cent. respectively. Among the children of skilled workers in South West Hertfordshire the proportion of awards to the group drawn from families of only one or two (21 per cent.) was almost twice as great as to that drawn from families of three or four (12 per cent.). In Middlesbrough the corresponding figures for the children of non-Catholic skilled workers were 19 and 12 per cent. respectively, and for children of even larger families of five or more at this social level the proportion of awards was only 5 per cent.

FAVOURABLE AND UNFAVOURABLE WORKING-CLASS HOMES

We have tried to go further into the influence of environment on success in the selection examination by a more detailed analysis of our information concerning the children of manual workers in the 10-11 age-group under study in each area. Although their parents form a comparatively homogeneous social group, working-class children, as we have seen, are reared under varied conditions at home and at school—in very old houses and in modern housing estates, in very poor and in very fine school buildings. Few children

---

[1] See Nisbet, J., *Family Environment*, Eugenics Society, 1953, for a comprehensive review of the relevant literature.
[2] See p. 134 below.

of non-manual workers live in poor material conditions at home, and there is less variety in the attitudes and preferences of their parents as to their education. The analysis therefore seemed likely to be more fruitful in the case of working-class children. Our object was to compare the influence on the success of working-class children in obtaining grammar school places of the material environment at school, the material environment at home, and the 'cultural' environment at home (as expressed in parents' education, attitudes and ambitions for their children). It is true that these are mutually reinforcing influences, difficult in practice to assess separately. Nevertheless the pace of post-war social reform has been uneven; school building is not always accompanied by rehousing and does not always serve the more prosperous and ambitious working-class families, and the spread of 'middle-class' attitudes in educational matters among working-class parents does not necessarily wait on improvements in their material environment. There is something to be gained, therefore, from an attempt to compare the relative strength of these influences on children's performance in the examination at 11+.

The relevant information was available in the case of 774 children of skilled and unskilled manual workers aged 10-11 in Middlesbrough, and 933 of the same group in South West Hertfordshire. These boys and girls were attending primary schools which were classified into three groups according to the condition of their buildings—'poor' (i.e. schools in Material Environment Categories 1 and 2), 'medium' (Category 3), and 'good' (Categories 4 and 5).[1] The children were further grouped according to an assessment, in simple quantitative terms, of the 'favourable' or 'unfavourable' material character of their home environment. Homes were awarded one mark in respect of each of the following characteristics: a 'good' basic income (i.e. senior wage-earner's income of more than £7 10s. per week); good

---

[1] cf. p. 71 above for a description of these 'categories'.

housing (i.e. a detached or semi-detached or council house); absence of overcrowding (i.e. at least one room per person); amenities (car, telephone, *or* television). The maximum score obtainable was thus 4; those homes with a total of 3 or 4 points were classified as 'favourable' and those with 0, 1 or 2 as 'unfavourable'.

A similar summary index was devised to express the favourable or unfavourable nature of parental views on educational matters. The following were each awarded one mark: at least one visit to the primary school in the course of the year of the enquiry for reasons connected with education, including the discussion of the child's secondary education with the Head Teacher or an assistant; a stated preference for some form of selective secondary education; the intention of keeping the child at school at least to the age of 16; the wish that the child should undergo some form of further education or training on leaving school. The classification of homes into 'favourable' and 'unfavourable' in this 'cultural' respect was likewise based on the size of the total score—3 or 4 'favourable', and 0, 1 or 2 'unfavourable'.

The distribution in each area of working-class homes rated 'favourable' or 'unfavourable' in either or both of these respects is shown in Table 22 (p. 107). The environmental handicap suffered by Middlesbrough children can be clearly seen. As many as 45 per cent. of the homes are rated 'wholly unfavourable' to the educational chances of the children living in them. The parents of one-third of the children in the sample, though interested in and ambitious for their educational future, are obliged to rear them in adverse material conditions. This environmental handicap must be partly responsible for the lower general rate of success on the part of Middlesbrough children from working-class families. The proportion obtaining grammar school places in 1953 was 12 per cent., compared with 15 per cent. in South West Hertfordshire in 1952. This difference is probably due to the slightly lower mean IQ of children of manual workers in Middlesbrough in the year of our enquiry, and to the rather fewer grammar school places. But the striking contrast in the material standards of their homes must be taken into account as an important factor determining the different chances of success for working-class children in the two areas.

The relation of the various kinds or qualities of home environment to the success of working-class children in obtaining grammar school places is shown in Table 23 (p. 108). Amongst the children whose homes are neither 'wholly favourable' nor 'wholly unfavourable', the rate of success was highest amongst those (group 2b in Table 23) whose parents are favourably disposed towards their educational prospects; the chances, especially in South West Hertfordshire, of children whose homes offer only material comfort (group 2a) were considerably less bright.

In Middlesbrough, more than half of the fathers of children in group 2b are in fact *unskilled* workers. Their families are more frequently restricted to one or two children than those in group 2a whose fathers are mainly skilled workers, more prosperous but less favourably disposed to the education of their children. Yet the average level of intelligence among children in group 2b is no higher than among those in 2a.[1] Their higher rate of success therefore represents the direct influence of the encouragement and interest of their parents. Moreover, one-third of these children were being educated in 'poor' schools. It seems reasonable to infer that any improvement in their material environment at home or school would result in a higher rate of success. Rehousing and new school buildings and modern

---

[1] The mean Intelligence Quotients are as follows:

	1 Home 'Wholly Favourable'	2a Material Environment Favourable	2b Parents' Attitudes Favourable	3 Home 'Wholly Unfavourable'
Middlesbrough	104·9	100·3	100·8	94·2
South West Hertfordshire	103·7	94·8	100·8	94·3

amenities could be expected to 'show results' fairly rapidly with this group of children.[1]

In South West Hertfordshire the situation of this group (2b) of children is rather different. A smaller but still sizeable proportion—some 40 per cent.—of the fathers are unskilled workers. There is a much stronger tendency than in Middlesbrough for their families to be smaller, and their mean IQ is substantially higher than that of children coming from families in the more prosperous group 2a.[2] They are about as likely to have been educated in a 'poor' as in a 'good' school. Evidently there is less scope than in Middlesbrough for improvement in these children's rate of success (23 per cent.), which in any case hardly differs from that of the group of children from homes rated 'wholly favourable' (21 per cent.). The material environment of homes must be heavily discounted as an influence on success in South West Hertfordshire where it is less varied than in Middlesbrough and of a better standard at all social levels.

THE INFLUENCE OF SCHOOL BUILDINGS

The marked differences in the rate at which the various primary schools of an area send pupils forward to grammar schools at the age of 11 are usually well-known to parents and have frequently been commented upon by investigators.[3]

In South West Hertfordshire in 1952, these differences were associated with the maintained or voluntary status of the schools, the age of the buildings in which they were housed, and the locality served by them. Thus, maintained primary schools sent forward an average of 21 per cent. of their 10-11 year old pupils to grammar schools, as compared

---

[1] See Glass, R. (ed.), op. cit., Part III, Ch. V, for evidence of the effect on success rates of improved school environment following the re-housing of families from North Middlesbrough. Also the further discussion of this point on pp. 98-9 below.

[2] See footnote p. 94.

[3] cf. for example, K. Lindsay, op. cit.; R. Glass, op. cit.

with 16 per cent. sent forward by the voluntary schools. All the voluntary schools were working in buildings constructed before 1901, and although the ratio of staff to pupils was higher than that in the maintained schools, they were more overcrowded and served populations of lower economic status. The character of the districts of the Division served by the schools was likewise reflected in their rate of success in the 11+ examination, the mean rate ranging, according to the district served, from 24 per cent. at one extreme to 12 per cent. at the other. Even within a single district, the differences between individual schools were just as marked, according to the wards they served. Thus, in the Borough of Watford, one school sent forward 47 per cent. of its candidates whilst another gained places for only 7 per cent. An analysis[1] which related rates of success in the competition for grammar school places to indices in turn of the material environment of the schools, the degree of their overcrowding and the economic status of the populations served by them showed the relation with the last variable to be closest.

This is not surprising; yet the relationship of the school buildings and amenities to the success of pupils in the selection tests at 11 is still worth exploring. Poor homes and poor schools are frequently associated.[2] Even within the same social class, poor homes imply a lower average level of measured intelligence amongst the children who are plainly unlikely to proceed to the grammar schools in the same proportion as those reared and educated under more favourable circumstances. It is likely that they will on the average score less well in intelligence tests, and also that their output at a given level of intelligence will be on the average inferior. But what is the effect of the post-war attempt to break this association by the construction of new

---

[1] See the unpublished thesis by A. H. Halsey, referred to p. 18 above, for a detailed exposition of the method and findings.

[2] See discussion of the association in Middlesbrough and South West Hertfordshire, p. 74 above.

primary schools to serve populations of low economic status, whether rehoused on new estates or not?

Table 24 (p. 108) sets out the proportions of working-class children sent to grammar schools from primary schools working in each of the three categories of material environment in Middlesbrough and South West Hertfordshire during the years of our enquiry. In neither area do the 'good' schools with working-class children show any outstanding rate of success. In South West Hertfordshire, the 'good' schools do as poorly in this respect as the 'poor' schools, and in Middlesbrough they share, without surpassing, the superiority of the 'medium' over the 'poor' schools.

It does not follow, however, that new school buildings can do nothing to improve the inferior chances which working-class children from poor homes have in the selection examination. If, in analysing the success of the different types of primary school with working-class children, we take account of the quality of their home background, the opportunities which the 'good' schools have to improve rates of success appear more favourable.

Table 25 (p. 109) gives a picture of the home background of the working-class children attending each type of primary school. It is noticeable that in both Middlesbrough and South West Hertfordshire there is in the 'good' schools a smaller proportion of pupils coming from homes which provide a material environment adverse to their parents' interests and ambitions for their education (Table 25, group 2b) than in either the 'medium' or the 'poor' schools, and a substantially higher proportion of pupils drawn from 'wholly favourable' homes. But as a result of movements of population, the 'good' schools also tend to have pupils drawn from homes which, before their (usually recent) transfer, would have been classed as 'unfavourable' from the point of view of material environment, but are now classed as 'favourable' in this respect; that is to say, they have a higher proportion of pupils from homes which are rated 'favourable' only as regards their material environment (group 2*a*). It is also worth remarking that one-quarter of the pupils attending 'poor' schools in South West Hertfordshire and one-third of the same group in Middlesbrough came from homes which, though not prosperous materially, were rated 'favourable' as regards their parents' attitudes to education; that is, favourably disposed and ambitious parents were not only rearing their children in poor conditions at home, but sending them to 'poor' primary schools.

The proportion of working-class children from different types of home background who proceed to grammar schools from each of the three grades of primary school in the two areas is shown in Table 26 (p. 110). It would be reasonable to expect that primary schools of all types would have most success with pupils from 'wholly favourable' homes; least success with those from 'wholly unfavourable' homes; and greater success with the children of educationally aware parents in poor circumstances than with those from merely comfortable homes. But obviously this pattern can only hold if the economic disabilities of educationally aware parents are not too severe. If we bear in mind the different parts played in Middlesbrough and South West Hertfordshire by material factors in children's examination performance at 11+ we shall not be surprised to find (Table 26, p. 110) that the expected pattern held in South West Hertfordshire for all types of school, but in Middlesbrough only for 'medium' or 'good' but not for 'poor' schools. In South West Hertfordshire, even when poor conditions at home were associated with poor conditions at school (i.e. in the case of working-class children attending 'poor' primary schools from homes classified as 'unfavourable' in respect of material environment) if parents' attitudes were 'favourable', they prevailed to produce a rate of success (19 per cent.) higher than that of children attending the same schools from more prosperous but less ambitious or enlightened homes (13 per cent.).

In Middlesbrough, on the other hand, the success of these children of educationally aware parents in poor material circumstances (14 per cent.) was lower than that of the children attending 'poor' schools whose homes were more comfortable though less favourably disposed in matters of education (23 per cent.); and it was lower than that achieved by children from this type of home in the 'medium' and 'good' schools (17 per cent.). It is not unreasonable to infer that the rehousing of the 'poor' schools would enable the children of poor but favourably disposed parents to improve their rate of success, and would do so to some extent even if the rehousing of the population did not go hand in hand with the rehousing of the schools.

Perhaps the best test of the influence of the 'good' schools is in respect of children whose homes were rated 'wholly unfavourable'. It will be noticed (Table 26, p. 110) that in South West Hertfordshire, though not in Middlesbrough, the 'good' schools show a rate of success for these children (1 per cent.) markedly inferior to that of 'poor' or 'medium' schools (8 per cent.). It must, however, be remembered that, whereas in Middlesbrough the category 'good' comprises established schools in pre-war buildings (with the exception of one post-war school, and a second to which children from the worst of the slum clearance areas in the centre of the town are transported daily by bus), in South West Hertfordshire five of the 'good' schools cater primarily for immigrant working-class families from London. The great majority of the children of these families have had their schooling disrupted in the confused conditions of post-war rehousing, and the new schools which they now attend have yet to develop the sort of tradition and character which gives the 'medium' schools, despite their relatively inferior buildings and amenities, their greater success with children from all types of home background.

Admittedly, a school is something more than bricks and mortar—but once it is well established with a tradition of its own, bricks and mortar are not to be despised. They enable more to be done for pupils from homes which are poor or educationally philistine, or both, than is possible under less favourable material conditions.

Table 14

SOCIAL DISTRIBUTION OF AWARDS OF GRAMMAR SCHOOL PLACES

	No. of Candidates			% successful (Col. 1 as % of Col. 3)
	Successful (1)	Unsuccessful (2)	All (3)	(4)
SOUTH WEST HERTFORDSHIRE (1952)				
Middle-Class				
Professional workers, business owners and managers ..	53	51	104	51
Lower Middle-Class				
Clerical workers	41	66	107	38
Foremen, small shopkeepers, etc.	57	198	255	22
	98	264	362	27
Working-Class				
Skilled	107	523	630	17
Unskilled	36	276	312	11
	143	799	942	15
All	294	1,114	1,408	21
MIDDLESBROUGH (1953)*				
Middle-Class				
Professional workers, business owners and managers ..	34	16	50	68
Lower Middle-Class				
Clerical workers	17	29	46	37
Foremen, small shopkeepers, etc.	33	104	137	24
	50	133	183	27
Working-Class				
Skilled	55	346	401	14
Unskilled	34	343	377	9
	89	689	778	12
All	173	838	1,011	17

* Including children from Roman Catholic primary schools.

Table 15

EDUCATION OF PARENTS OF SUCCESSFUL AND UNSUCCESSFUL CANDIDATES FOR GRAMMAR SCHOOL PLACES

	Father's Education				Mother's Education			
	Selective Secondary		Some Further Education		Selective Secondary		Some Further Education	
	S*	U*	S	U	S	U	S	U
	%	%	%	%	%	%	%	%
SOUTH WEST HERTFORDSHIRE (1952)								
Middle-Class	85	36	77	63	83	63	49	26
Lower Middle-Class	49	36	44	41	51	32	50	10
Working-Class	14	10	32	18	31	14	22	13
All	38	17	45	25	44	20	31	18
MIDDLESBROUGH (1953)								
Middle-Class	88	56	85	70	65	50	56	38
Lower Middle-Class	40	17	48	28	36	14	28	17
Working-Class	8	6	25	12	11	3	12	7
All	33	8	43	15	29	6	25	9

S and U indicate successful and unsuccessful children respectively. The numbers on which the percentages are based may be found in Table 14, p. 100.

Table 16

ATTITUDES AND PREFERENCES OF PARENTS OF SUCCESSFUL AND UNSUCCESSFUL CANDIDATES FOR GRAMMAR SCHOOL PLACES

	'Preference' for Grammar School		'Strong Preference' for Grammar School		Have discussed child's secondary education with Primary teachers		Contemplate leaving age of 18		Desire child to have Further Education or Training	
	S*	U*	S	U	S	U	S	U	S	U
	%	%	%	%	%	%	%	%	%	%
SOUTH WEST HERTFORDSHIRE (1952)										
Middle-Class	81	82	68	63	71	55	79	51	83	78
Lower Middle-Class	84	58	68	61	72	57	51	27	53	57
Working-Class	80	41	51	21	59	30	44	16	47	44
All	81	47	56	27	69	40	53	20	52	49
MIDDLESBROUGH (1953)										
Middle-Class	97	81	88	87	71	63	74	44	91	75
Lower Middle-Class	86	57	66	33	98	56	44	25	60	51
Working-Class	80	44	57	22	54	31	33	15	44	45
All	85	47	66	26	62	29	44	17	58	49

* S and U indicate successful and unsuccessful children respectively. The numbers on which percentages are based may be found in Table 14, p. 100.

Table 17

MATERIAL PROSPERITY OF HOMES OF SUCCESSFUL AND UNSUCCESSFUL CANDIDATES FOR GRAMMAR SCHOOL PLACES

	% Families			
	Chief wage-earner's income rated 'high'†		Occupying detached or semi-detached house	
	S*	U*	S	U
SOUTH WEST HERTFORDSHIRE (1952)				
Middle-Class	53	61	83	86
Lower Middle-Class	43	44	73	75
Working-Class	48	47	59	64
All	46	47	66	68
MIDDLESBROUGH (1953)				
Middle-Class	41	38	79	44
Lower Middle-Class	38	24	46	35
Working Class	63	45	26	18
All	51	41	42	21

* S and U indicate successful and unsuccessful children respectively. The numbers on which the percentages are based may be found in Table 14, p. 100.

† The definition of 'high' income varied according to social class. Thus: Middle-Class £15 or over p.w. Lower Middle-Class £10 or over p.w. Working-Class £7 10s. or over p.w.

Table 18

AWARDS OF GRAMMAR SCHOOL PLACES IN RELATION TO THE MATERIAL PROSPERITY OF CHILDREN'S HOMES

% awarded Grammar School places

	Income of Chief Wage-earner		Housing	
	High*	Low	Detached or Semi-detached	Terraced
SOUTH WEST HERTFORDSHIRE (1952)				
Middle and Lower Middle-Class	34 (208)	31 (194)	37 (357)	30 (64)
Working-Class:				
Skilled	19 (378)	16 (213)	16 (416)	17 (153)
Unskilled	9 (81)	13 (215)	10 (177)	14 (105)
All	22 (667)	20 (622)	21 (950)	19 (322)
MIDDLESBROUGH (1953)				
Middle and Lower Middle-Class ..	44 (70)	32 (130)	49 (104)	25 (123)
Working-Class:				
Skilled	18 (234)	9 (137)	22 (99)	11 (289)
Unskilled	11 (129)	8 (210)	23 (43)	10 (327)
All	20 (433)	15 (477)	30 (246)	13 (739)

* *The definition of 'high' income varies according to social class. See footnote to Table 17, p. 103.*
NOTE: Percentages are based on the numbers shown in brackets. In the case of MIDDLESBROUGH these represent a 50% sample of the age-group.

Table 19

AWARDS OF GRAMMAR SCHOOL PLACES IN RELATION TO EDUCATION OF CHILDREN'S PARENTS

% awarded Grammar School places

	Father's Education				Mother's Education			
	Secondary		Further		Secondary		Further	
	Selective	Other	Some	None	Selective	Other	Some	None
SOUTH WEST HERTFORDSHIRE (1952)								
Middle and Lower Middle-Class	42 (205)	24 (231)	38 (223)	28 (244)	45 (211)	22 (256)	36 (172)	30 (308)
Working-Class:								
Skilled	21 (82)	16 (541)	26 (160)	14 (472)	26 (107)	15 (525)	26 (104)	15 (531)
Unskilled	13 (23)	12 (286)	22 (27)	11 (286)	13 (62)	11 (251)	19 (26)	11 (287)
All	34 (310)	17 (1058)	40 (410)	16 (1002)	34 (380)	16 (1032)	32 (302)	18 (1126)
MIDDLESBROUGH (1953)								
Middle and Lower Middle-Class	61 (82)	22 (150)	52 (103)	23 (130)	61 (66)	24 (165)	25 (59)	29 (169)
Working-Class:								
Skilled	19 (32)	13 (365)	25 (87)	11 (320)	36 (25)	12 (369)	24 (37)	12 (353)
Unskilled	8 (13)	9 (360)	10 (21)	1 (353)	11 (9)	1 (362)	11 (18)	9 (355)
All	45 (127)	13 (875)	37 (202)	12 (803)	50 (100)	14 (896)	38 (114)	14 (877)

NOTE: The numbers on which percentages are based are shown in brackets. In the case of MIDDLESBOROUGH these are based on a 50% sample of the age-group.

Table 20

AWARDS OF GRAMMAR SCHOOL PLACES IN RELATION TO THE ATTITUDES OF CHILDREN'S PARENTS TO THEIR EDUCATION

% awarded Grammar School places

	Discussed child's secondary education with primary teacher		Preference for Grammar Secondary		School-leaving age preferred			Further education or training desired	
	Yes	No	Grammar School	Modern School	18+	16-17	15	Some	None
SOUTH WEST HERTFORDSHIRE									
Middle and Lower Middle-Class ..	38 (287)	20 (179)	47 (322)	19 (145)	49 (188)	28 (188)	7 (81)	35 (282)	29 (185)
Working-Class:									
Skilled	27 (268)	10 (364)	29 (304)	6 (328)	35 (145)	16 (250)	6 (226)	18 (301)	29 (180)
Unskilled ..	22 (95)	7 (217)	21 (135)	4 (178)	27 (44)	17 (102)	3 (159)	13 (133)	4 (199)
All	31 (650)	12 (760)	31 (761)	8 (651)	41 (377)	21 (540)	5 (466)	31 (716)	15 (564)
MIDDLESBROUGH									
Middle and Lower Middle-Class ..	39 (142)	27 (191)	46 (165)	11 (68)	52 (90)	29 (98)	17 (41)	43 (141)	23 (92)
Working-Class:									
Skilled ..	16 (145)	8 (253)	22 (200)	6 (198)	27 (81)	16 (144)	5 (161)	10 (199)	17 (199)
Unskilled ..	10 (118)	6 (259)	16 (175)	3 (202)	15 (48)	14 (132)	5 (189)	11 (167)	7 (210)
All	20 (405)	9 (603)	27 (540)	6 (468)	35 (219)	19 (374)	6 (391)	20 (507)	15 (501)

NOTE: The numbers on which percentages are based are shown in brackets. In the case of MIDDLESBROUGH these are based on a 50% sample of the age-group.

Table 21

AWARDS OF GRAMMAR SCHOOL PLACES IN RELATION TO FAMILY
SIZE

	% awarded grammar school places No. of Children in Family		
	1–2	3–4	5+
SOUTH WEST HERTFORDSHIRE (1952)			
Middle and Lower Middle-Class	35 (255)	31 (169)	21 (42)
Working-Class: Skilled ..	21 (277)	12 (245)	17 (108)
Unskilled ..	17 (122)	11 (126)	2 (64)
All	26 (654)	18 (540)	13 (214)
MIDDLESBROUGH (1953)			
Middle and Lower Middle-Class	43 (103)	28 (71)	20 (20)
Working-Class: Skilled ..	19 (115)	12 (133)	5 (75)
Unskilled ..	9 (86)	7 (109)	3 (87)
All	24 (304)	14 (313)	6 (182)

NOTE: The numbers on which percentages are based are shown in
brackets. In the case of MIDDLESBROUGH these are based on a 50%
sample of the age-group excluding children attending Roman
Catholic Primary Schools, for which see p. 137 below.

Table 22

HOME ENVIRONMENT OF WORKING-CLASS CHILDREN

Home Environment	South West Hertfordshire %	Middlesbrough %
1. Wholly favourable	27	13
2. One aspect favourable only		
(a) Environment	20	9
(b) Attitudes	25	33
3. Wholly unfavourable	28	45
Total	100	100
(N)	(933)	(774)*

* This figure represents a 50% sample of the age-group of working-
class children, excluding those from Roman Catholic families, for which
see p. 137 below.

Table 23

AWARDS OF GRAMMAR SCHOOL PLACES TO WORKING-CLASS CHILDREN FROM DIFFERENT TYPES OF HOME

Home Environment	% awarded places in Grammar Schools	
	South West Hertfordshire (1952)	Middlesbrough* (1953)
1. Wholly favourable	21	24
2. One aspect favourable only (a) Environment	9	12
(b) Attitudes	23	15
3. Wholly unfavourable	6	5
All types of home	15	12

* *Excluding children from Roman Catholic families, for which see p. 138 below.*

Table 24

AWARDS OF GRAMMAR SCHOOL PLACES TO WORKING CLASS CHILDREN IN DIFFERENT TYPES OF PRIMARY SCHOOL

Material Environment of Primary School†	% awarded places in Grammar Schools	
	South West Hertfordshire (1952)	Middlesbrough* (1953)
Poor	14	9
Medium	22	14
Good	13	14
All types of school	15	12

* *Excluding children of Roman Catholic families.*
† *See p. 92 above.*

Table 25

HOME ENVIRONMENT OF WORKING-CLASS CHILDREN ATTENDING
DIFFERENT TYPES OF PRIMARY SCHOOL

Home Environment	Type of Primary School		
	'Poor'	'Medium'	'Good'
	%	%	%
SOUTH WEST HERTFORDSHIRE			
(1) Wholly favourable	20	23	35
(2) One aspect favourable only			
(a) Environment	18	13	25
(b) Attitudes	25	37	19
(3) Wholly unfavourable	37	27	21
Total	100	100	100
(N)	340	176	417
MIDDLESBROUGH			
(1) Wholly favourable	4	15	24
(2) One aspect favourable only			
(a) Environment	4	11	14
(b) Attitudes	33	39	27
(3) Wholly unfavourable	59	35	35
Total	100	100	100
(N)*	350	196	228

These figures are based on a 50% sample of the age-group of working-class children, excluding those from Roman Catholic families.

Table 26

SUCCESS OF DIFFERENT TYPES OF PRIMARY SCHOOL WITH
WORKING-CLASS CHILDREN OF VARYING HOME BACKGROUND

Home Environment	*Type of Primary School*		
	'Poor' %	'Medium' %	'Good' %
SOUTH WEST HERTFORDSHIRE (1952)			
(1) Wholly favourable	20 (68)	28 (40)	20 (142)
(2) One aspect favourable only			
(*a*) Environment ..	13 (62)	13 (23)	7 (105)
(*b*) Attitudes	19 (85)	32 (65)	20 (81)
(3) Wholly unfavourable ..	8 (125)	8 (48)	1 (89)
Total	14 (340)	22 (176)	13 (417)
MIDDLESBROUGH (1953)			
(1) Wholly favourable	25 (16)	17 (30)	28 (54)
(2) One aspect favourable only			
(*a*) Environment ..	23 (13)	14 (22)	6 (33)
(*b*) Attitudes	14 (115)	17 (76)	17 (62)
(3) Wholly unfavourable ..	4 (206)	4 (68)	5 (79)
Total	9 (350)	14 (196)	14 (228)

NOTE. The numbers on which the percentages are based are shown in
brackets. In the case of MIDDLESBROUGH these are based on a
50% sample of the age-groups of working-class children, excluding
those from Roman Catholic families, for which see p. 138 below.

ACHIEVEMENT IN SCHOOL AND SOCIAL
CLASS

WE HAVE been discussing the influence of the social origins and home background of children on their chances of being selected at the age of 11 for admission to a grammar school. It remains now to follow them into the secondary schools and to observe the continuing influence of these factors on their achievements there. In this first stage of our investigation we have confined our attention to the select minority who enter grammar schools in order to discover what use they are able to make of this educational opportunity. It is well known that up to 60 per cent. of them leave the grammar schools before they are 17. This is generally deplored. But, before we can assess this problem, we need to know something about the changes which have taken place over the past half-century in the average length of school life. We also need to know how far this and the related problem of poor school performance represent a process of *social* rather than purely academic selection within the schools.

Information was collected on the length of school life and on the success in public examinations of entrants to grammar schools in various years since 1884, and some information on the destiny of leavers in selected years during the 1930's and after 1945. The problem can thus be set in its historical context, comparing local developments with the national developments revealed in the annual reports of the Board and Ministry of Education since 1900.[1] It is then possible to relate the length of school life and the academic achievements of pupils to their social origins, and to make a tentative enquiry into the influence of the distribution of ability on this process of selection within the schools.

---

[1] Discussion of local developments relates to boys only. The information concerning girls which was collected in South West Hertfordshire is presented in Halsey, A. H., op. cit.

As this book was in preparation, the problem of early leaving from grammar schools was investigated on a national scale by the Central Advisory Council for Education.[1] It has now been established beyond doubt that there is a process of social as well as academic selection at work in the schools. The discussion which follows presents the historical background in more detail and shows the trend of local developments in the areas under study.

---

[1] Central Advisory Council for Education (England). *Early Leaving*. H.M.S.O., 1954.

CHAPTER 7

LENGTH OF SCHOOL LIFE, PUBLIC EXAMINATIONS AND FULL-TIME FURTHER EDUCATION

LENGTH OF SCHOOL LIFE

THE ACHIEVEMENTS rather than the shortcomings of the post-war educational revolution were emphasized in earlier chapters, and particularly the transformation of public opinion on the length of school life.[1] This emphasis is justified by the great change which has taken place over the past 40 years, both nationally and in the areas of our enquiry, in the age at which children, particularly from the better-off classes, normally leave the secondary schools.

The national picture

For the country as a whole we have the information given in the Annual Reports of the Board and Ministry of Education on the leaving ages of fee-paying and free-place pupils respectively. It is clear that until the late 1930's, fee-paying pupils consistently left school at an earlier age than did those who held free places. But the difference in the average age at which the two groups left school gradually narrowed until it closed in 1938 at 16 years 7 months.[2] It is true that the Central Advisory Council draws attention in its recent report to 'a clear and continuous tendency towards a *shorter* school life in the pre-war years for which figures are available'.[3] But, as the Report indicates, the figures relate to children who entered grammar schools in the period 1927-30 and therefore reached the age of 15 at a time of economic

---

[1] See Chapter 5 above.
[2] *Education in 1938*. Cmd. 6013 (our italics).
[3] op. cit., pp. 5-6.

depression in the years 1931-34. The figures shown in Table 27 below[1] suggest that the shortening of school life in these years interrupted a well-established long-term trend in the opposite direction. The tendency towards a longer school life which has been so marked a feature of the post-war years resumes the long-term trend and may be expected to continue unless interrupted, as in the 1930's, by economic vicissitude.

There are, in fact, two distinct problems—one of *premature* and the other of *early* leaving. 'Premature' leavers are pupils who leave as soon as they are legally able, or shortly after, but in any case before the completion of the grammar school course; 'early' leavers are pupils who stay at school until the end of the five-year course (i.e. usually until 16), but do not enter the sixth form—and there are some amongst them who do not even obtain a school leaving certificate.[2]

Premature leaving, as Table 27 (p. 128) shows, has declined steadily since the beginning of the century among both fee-payers and free-place pupils, but in the period 1935-38 it was most frequent amongst children paying part-fees under the Special Place Regulations of 1933. These children must have come mainly from lower middle-class families. 'Ordinary' fee-payers, presumably for the most part of middle-class origin, and Special Place pupils whose parents were not required to pay fees, no doubt mainly of working-class origin, showed less tendency to leave before completing the course.

Besides the reduction of premature leaving, the increased average length of school life also reflects an increased proportion of pupils staying at school beyond their seven-

---

[1] p. 128. These figures relate to *leavers* from grammar schools in various years and are therefore not directly comparable with those in Table A of the Council's Report, which relate to *entrants*.

[2] It is perhaps worth pointing out that a small number of premature leavers, on the other hand, may have left with a School Certificate obtained at the age of 15 or even 14. Age of leaving is only a rough criterion of 'wastage'.

teenth (and eighteenth) birthday, as may be seen from Table 28 (p. 129) (though in the years between 1925 and 1939 this was not true of girls holding free or special places).

It is noticeable that until the mid-'twenties, a larger proportion of free-place holders than of fee-payers remained at school to the age of 17 or over. The question evidently turned on academic quality; the able, because selected, minority stayed on, and the rest tended to leave. The relation between the two groups in this respect changed, however, in the mid-'thirties when public appreciation of the value of a longer school life grew. Those who could afford to do so stayed on to enter the Sixth Form, with the result that the proportion of late-leaving fee-paying pupils began to rise. The long-term trend towards intensified competition for black-coated and professional employment was already making itself felt in the middle twenties, and the minimum qualifications for entry to these occupations were being raised. The economic depression later also played its part in keeping some boys at secondary school after the age of 16 in the hope that opportunities for employment would improve before they were compelled to find jobs 'below their schooling'.

But the problem of *early leaving* remains, and has become of greater relative importance as premature leaving has declined, as can be seen from Table 29 (p. 130), which shows the change in the proportion of children leaving at the age of 16.

Since the war the tendency towards a longer school life has been very marked. As many as 20 per cent. of the children who entered grammar schools in 1947 stayed at school until after their 18th birthday, as compared with 15 per cent. of those who entered in 1945.[1] It is worth remarking, however, that although the proportions of premature and early leavers are smaller than they were, the absolute numbers of both are considerably greater owing to

---

[1] Central Advisory Council, op. cit., Table A, p. 5.

the expansion of secondary education since 1944; the problem therefore remains acute both for the schools and from
the point of view of the loss of qualified man-power to the
national economy.

The Local Picture

Our information for South West Hertfordshire and Middlesbrough is derived from school records of varying quality
and relates to boys only.[1] The national pattern holds in both
areas, though the distinction between scholars and fee-payers
is more marked in South West Hertfordshire than in
Middlesbrough. Until the middle thirties boys holding free
places had, on the average, a longer school life than those
paying fees. They were less inclined to leave school before
the age of 16 and more inclined to stay on at least until 17
(Table 30, p. 131). There was the same marked tendency in
the middle thirties for fee-payers to lengthen their school life,
and this was particularly striking in South West Hertfordshire; in the period 1934-38 the proportion of fee-paying
boys staying at school to the age of 17 or over was half as
great again (44 per cent.) as that of free-place holders (28 per
cent.).

If the categories 'free-place holder' and 'fee-payer' are
sub-divided in terms of social origins, though the numbers
in each occupational group are very small, it is clear that
in both areas, with insignificant exceptions in the earlier
years, the higher incidence of premature leaving amongst
fee-payers applied to boys at all social levels. On the other
hand we find that in both areas, *within* the selected minority
of free-place holders, the sons of middle-class families
tended to have longer school lives than their fellows from
working-class families. With few exceptions, the proportion
of free-place holders leaving under 16 decreases with each

---

[1] Less complete information was available concerning girls and is set
out for South West Hertfordshire in the unpublished Ph.D. thesis by
A. H. Halsey, op. cit.

step up the occupational scale, whilst the proportion of those remaining at school until 17 or over increases.

The post-war position is compared with that of the pre-war period in Table 31 (p. 132). Since 1945 there have been no fee-payers in the schools, and the proportion of boys leaving before the age of 16 has fallen to half the pre-war figure. Thus, in 1935-38 it was 22 per cent. in South West Hertfordshire and 24 per cent. in Middlesbrough, whilst in both areas during the period 1948-51 it amounted only to some 12 per cent., which also compared very favourably with the national average at that time.[1] It is worth noting that this reduction in premature leaving is spread fairly evenly in Middlesbrough over the social groups and is particularly striking in the case of working-class boys (from 33 per cent. in 1935-38 to 15 per cent. in 1948-51). In South West Hertfordshire, however, the sons of manual workers continue to leave school before they are 16 in much the same proportion (some 20 per cent.) as before the war, and the reduction has been most striking in the case of lower middle-class boys (i.e. the sons of clerks, shopkeepers, etc., 29 per cent. of whom left before the age of 16 in 1935-38 as compared with only 10 per cent. in 1948-51).

In South West Hertfordshire the proportion of boys staying at school until the age of 17 or over has risen substantially since the war—54 per cent. in 1948-51 as against 39 per cent. in 1934-38. There has, however, been no comparable increase in Middlesbrough—the figure for 1948-50 was 28 per cent. compared with 25 per cent. in 1935-37. In both areas the lengthening of the school life of the sons of clerical workers is particularly noticeable. In 1948-50 the proportion of boys from this group of Middlesbrough families staying on till the later ages (43 per cent.) was almost double the 1935-37 figure (24 per cent.), and although in South West Hertfordshire the expansion of the sixth form was more evenly spread among the various social groups,

---

[1] In 1948 the figure for England and Wales, boys and girls, was 23%, and in 1951, 20%. (Annual Reports, Ministry of Education.)

the sons of clerical workers still stood out as proportionately the largest contributors to it (in 1935-38, 39 per cent. left at the age of 17 or over; in 1948-50 they were 65 per cent.).

In neither area, however, has there been any reduction of the difference between the 'chances' of boys of different social origins remaining at school until 17 or over. A professional or managerial worker's son in Middlesbrough was still in 1948-50, as in 1935-37, more than twice as likely as the son of a manual worker to remain at school after the completion of the minimum course. In South West Hertfordshire, although the rather wider pre-war difference between the chances of the sons of the middle and working-classes respectively has been slightly narrowed, the son of professional or business parents is still, as in Middlesbrough, more than twice as likely to enter the sixth form.

The problem of *premature* leaving is, as we have seen, being tackled. The problem of *early* leaving is still acute, partly on account of the rise in the academic demands of the secondary schools and in the length of the course considered desirable. The number of 17-year-old pupils in the grammar schools throughout the country has doubled since the war. However, the great diminution of social discrimination at the moment of entry to the schools has given them a social composition much more representative of the general population, and since the staying power of children in the face of the now lengthened and stiffened secondary course varies according to their social origins to roughly the same degree as formerly, the problem of 'early' leaving remains acute.

PUBLIC EXAMINATIONS AND ENTRY TO A UNIVERSITY

Between the wars, in the country as a whole, boys holding free places not only had on the average a longer school life than fee-paying pupils, but greater academic success. In 1938, as the following figures show,[1] they gained School and

---

[1] Proportion of Leavers (boys) from Secondary Schools on the Grant List who obtained certificates and proceeded to universities. The figures are for England and Wales. See *Education in 1938*. Cmd. 6013.

Higher School Certificates and proceeded to universities and other institutions of full-time education, in proportionately greater numbers than fee-paying pupils.

Fees paid		Total number of leavers	% obtaining School Certificate	Higher School Certificate	% Proceeding to University
Full fees	..	19,223	43·3	4·8	6·0
Part fees	..	2,457	52·5	5·3	4·7
No fees	..	21,548	63·2	11·5	7·4
Total	..	43,228	53·8	8·2	6·6

The pattern in Middlesbrough and South West Hertfordshire was not quite so satisfactory after 1935. Although in both areas the superiority of the boys holding free places held good up to School Certificate level (and even, in South West Hertfordshire, up to Higher School Certificate level), fee-payers were in the ascendant from that point onwards. In both areas, as the following figures for the years immediately before the war[1] show, proportionately more fee-payers than free-place holders went on to universities and other institutions of full-time further education. In Middlesbrough the two groups were much more evenly matched in the proportions proceeding to universities but the general proportion of university entrants was much smaller (5 per cent.) than in South West Hertfordshire (9 per cent.).

	No. of leavers (excl. pupils transferred to other areas)		% obtaining School Certificate		Higher School Certificate		% proceeding to University		Other full time further education	
	S	F	S	F	S	F	S	F	S	F
S.W. Herts.	89	177	87	70	15	11	1	14	1	5
*Middlesbrough	183	111	72	59	5	5	4	5	1	9

S—free and special place holders.
F—fee paying pupils.

* Excluding boys attending Roman Catholic Grammar Schools.

---

[1] South West Hertfordshire, 1935-8; Middlesbrough, 1935-7.

The pre-war and post-war situations are compared in Table 32 (p. 133). Since the war, the proportion of all boys leaving with School Certificate has increased in both areas and the proportion leaving with Higher School Certificate is more than three times as great. The proportion of boys entering universities from South West Hertfordshire has doubled, and that from Middlesbrough has trebled. However, the proportion of boys of *working-class origin* leaving with School Certificate has barely changed in either area; the gap which existed before the war in Middlesbrough, between the record of achievement in the School Certificate examination of the sons of professional and business parents and that of the sons of working-class parents has been widened whilst in South West Hertfordshire such a gap has appeared for the first time. Thus, the great improvement already noticed in the proportion of working-class boys remaining at school beyond the age of compulsory attendance has not resulted in a greater proportion of them completing the grammar school course in the approved way by obtaining a leaving certificate. In fact, as a group, they are primarily responsible for the size of the hard core of pupils who leave without a certificate.

In each area about twice as high a proportion of working-class boys as before the war take Higher School Certificate. But whereas before the war there were in neither area any notable class differences in the proportion of boys taking Higher School Certificate (the proportion in 1934-38 was virtually the same at all social levels, and small in any case), on the other hand from 1948-50, for which years comparable figures are available, the class differences were very marked in both areas. In South West Hertfordshire more than half of the sons of professional and business men and more than one-third of the lower middle-class boys left with Higher School Certificates, as compared with only just over a quarter of the working-class boys. In Middlesbrough the relevant proportions were one-third, one-fifth, and 13 per cent. respectively.

Those working-class boys who stay to take the Higher School Certificate have a much greater chance of proceeding to a university—six times as great in South West Hertfordshire, where it took the 1944 Education Act to bring about any effective change in the opportunities of working-class children, and twice as great in Middlesbrough. But the chances that a boy from a professional or business family would reach a university were in 1948-50 still twice as great in South West Hertfordshire and almost three times as great in Middlesbrough, although it is worth noting that this increase at the university level is no greater than that already noted at the Higher School Certificate level. That is to say, social as distinct from academic selection is at work at the threshold of the Sixth Form, but is not at work to any extent worth noting (in these two areas) at the point of entry to the university for those who manage to secure the necessary qualifications.

Determined boys do not suffer handicaps comparable with those endured by their forebears in the secondary schools between the wars. The problem is, however, to discover amongst those who leave at each stage beyond the age of compulsory attendance, the able boys who are apparently not 'determined'. It is important to know whether they are to be found in any number which would suggest the influence of other than random and idiosyncratic factors.

ABILITY AND ACHIEVEMENT IN GRAMMAR SCHOOLS

The question now arises as to the part played by the distribution of ability in this process of selection within the grammar school itself. As has already been shown, both in Middlesbrough and South West Hertfordshire there are small but significant differences, even within the selected population of the grammar school, in the mean IQ's of children from families in the different occupational groups —the children of manual workers gaining on the average the lowest score. It is to be expected, therefore, that a smaller

proportion of these children will be qualified to enter the
Sixth Form and to proceed to full-time further education.
The fact that such a relatively high proportion of them are
'early leavers' no doubt reflects their lower average level
of measured intelligence. It also reflects the general handicap
to a grammar school pupil of a working-class, rather than a
middle-class home background. We must ask, nevertheless:
Is it in fact the case that the children, particularly the
working-class children, who leave grammar schools at the
threshold of the Sixth Form have already approached their
'academic ceiling'? Or would they benefit from a Sixth Form
course, and are there potential graduates amongst them?
Opinion varies because local conditions vary.[1] But there can
be no doubt of the wastage on a national scale. From a study
of the grammar school intake of 1946 the Central Advisory
Council concludes that about 5,000 boys and 5,000 girls had
the capacity to take advanced Sixth Form courses, but left
school before doing so. 'If all these boys and girls had
completed advanced courses, the number of boys who in
fact did so would have been increased by about half and the
number of girls by about two-thirds.'[2] This finding is based
on an analysis of the judgments of the Heads of a representative 10 per cent. sample of English grammar schools,
and these judgments probably represent the best available
criterion of capacity for Sixth Form work. Measured
intelligence is a poor substitute, but we have used it as the

---

[1] Thus, in the opinion of R. Dale, who in his *From School to University* (Kegan Paul, 1954) gathers together evidence from a number of
small investigations, 'there is little doubt that the grammar schools
still have a not unimportant reserve of potential university students'
and the largest reserve is amongst pupils who leave early. This is
contrary to the view of the Head Master of Watford Grammar School
for Boys, who stated in a letter to *The Times Educational Supplement*,
16th October, 1953, 'the huge majority (of those who leave after taking
the ordinary level of the General Certificate of Education) have approached their academic ceiling, and to ask them to continue (with
sixth form studies) would be a waste of time. There are very few
potential graduates leaving the grammar school at sixteen.'
[2] Central Advisory Council, op. cit., p. 59.

criterion in a tentative attempt to estimate the extent of the problem in relation to boys in the grammar schools of South West Hertfordshire and Middlesbrough. It has the advantage that it offers a precise basis for comparing the actual with the potential school performance of children of differing social origins. There is no reason to suppose that a working-class boy who can achieve an IQ of 125 at the age of 11 *need* be nearer his academic ceiling at the age of 16 than the similarly qualified boy of professional or business parentage. The fact that he *is* so needs investigating.

The relation of wastage to social class in Middlesbrough may be illustrated by what we know of the only group of boys who entered grammar schools after 1945 and have already completed the minimum course at the age of 16. In this group of 1946 entrants as a whole there were 65 working-class boys and of these only 5 reached the Sixth Form. Sixteen of the 40 lower middle-class boys did so, and 5 of the 15 from professional and business families. There are, of course, the differences in the mean IQ's of the children according to their social origins. But these are very small, particularly as between manual workers' children and those of foremen, small shopkeepers, etc., and yet nearly half of this latter group went into the Sixth Form.

If the destinies at 16 of the 44 boys in this group with IQ's of 125 or more are examined separately, we find that of 19 working-class boys at this level of ability *only one* entered the Sixth Form, whereas half the total of 25 boys from lower middle-class and middle-class families did so. On the other hand only 2 of the whole group of 44 able boys left on reaching the age of 15, and of those leaving at 16, the great majority entered apprenticeships (in which there is, of course, no reason *prima facie* to suppose that their ability would be wasted).

The information available concerning the school careers of a group of boys with IQ's of 125 or more who left grammar schools in South West Hertfordshire in 1952-53 is not exactly comparable, but has very similar implications.

Nine of the 10 boys whose fathers were professional or business men had entered the Sixth Form; so had 15 of the 22 boys of lower middle-class origins. But only 7 of the 15 whose fathers were manual workers had done so.

It is clear that children at a given level of ability above the average are more or less likely to undertake advanced courses and go on to full-time further education according to their social origins. But it is also clear that the wider social significance of early leaving at a given level of ability demands discussion in the light of local conditions. Thus, between South West Hertfordshire and Middlesbrough there are striking differences in local tradition in regard to length of school life and full-time further education.[1]

Throughout the inter-war period the incidence of premature and early leaving amongst boys was noticeably heavier in Middlesbrough than in South West Hertfordshire, especially amongst free place pupils. This no doubt reflected the generally poorer economic conditions in Middlesbrough. But since in all occupational groups the incidence of premature leaving was greater than in South West Hertfordshire, it must have been at least partly due to local interest in industrial apprenticeship which could not be entered after the age of 16.[2]

The prospects of a technical career in industry are often very good for the Middlesbrough Grammar School boy of 16, and advanced work at school does not necessarily attract him. He has the chance of being accepted as a technical, or even as a craft apprentice, with good prospects ahead. But if he remains at school and yet fails to get into a university or technical college, he has missed his opportunity of becoming a trainee

---

[1] See pp. 118-123 above.
[2] Only in 1953 was agreement reached between the N.E. Coast Iron and Steel Trades Allied Craftsmen Committee and the N.E. Coast Steel Employers on the raising of the upper age limit to 17. Some other industries also are now prepared to consider boys for apprenticeship up to the age of 17 years.

technician.[1] Two years in the Sixth Form have considerable market value, however, for boys who will enter the large commercial and industrial concerns, banks, the Civil Service or the Armed Forces. There is little question of the able boy in South West Hertfordshire 'missing chances' by not leaving school at 16. On the contrary, the demand today for 'good' boys of 17 and 18 in non-technical jobs greatly enhances the value of Sixth Form education as an approach to a career.[2]

If the extent to which early leaving represents 'wastage' is to be properly assessed, considerations of this kind must be taken into account. However, if ability at a given level can best be realized after advanced work at school or at a university, the motives which prevent its realization must be discovered and combated. Parents' intentions and ambitions for their children when they are young may prove to be less important factors than disillusionment with the grammar school course or the attraction of local opportunities for employment combined with training and further education 'on the job'. Only the systematic and intensive study of children's performance in secondary schools of all types in relation to their home circumstances can throw light on the working and wider significance of the process of social selection in the grammar schools.

---

[1] Grammar School boys are in demand as trainee technicians in the iron and steel industry. Boys are recruited by examination for training in drawing offices and as metallurgical chemists and fuel engineers. In September 1952 the total intake of technical apprentices to an important local concern was 43. Of these, 31 came from grammar schools and 12 from the technical school. The Middlesbrough Education Committee's Annual Report on Youth Employment for 1950-1 remarks, 'the desire for a craft apprenticeship has now completely superseded the former attraction of a "white-collar" job' and attributes this to 'the greater attention which is now paid in industry to the training of the young entrants'. The Report further states that 'Grammar School boys have shown great interest and enthusiasm for posts as draughtsmen, so much so that at examinations conducted by local iron and steel and constructional engineering firms it is known that at least 150 boys competed for posts'.

[2] cf. in this connection the remarks of the Chairman of the Careers and Public Relations Committee, I.A.H.M., in *The Times Educational Supplement*, 26.6.54.

Table 27

PROPORTION OF PUPILS LEAVING SECONDARY (GRAMMAR) SCHOOLS *UNDER THE AGE OF 16 YEARS*, ENGLAND AND WALES (1910-1953)[1]

	1910-1913 (England only) %	1921 %	1926-1930 %	1935-1938 %	1948-1950 %	1951-1953 %
Free and Special Place Holders						
Boys	55·9	48·7	30·6	28·2	24·2	16·6
Girls	31·7	33·4	27·3	26·0	25·8	19·6
Fee-Paying Pupils						
Boys	67·4	61·6	40·2	29·6 (32·9)	—	—
Girls	57·6	59·2	40·6	34·0 (37·7)	—	—

[1] *Compiled from the Annual Reports of the Board (Ministry) of Education.*

NOTES: 1921. The only year in the period 1921-25 when the returns distinguish free place holders from fee-paying pupils.

Up to 1928, leavers aged 12-15 are included.

1929 and after, only leavers aged 14 and 15 are included.

1935-38. Part fee-payers in brackets.

1948 and after. Direct Grant grammar schools excluded.

Table 28

PROPORTION OF PUPILS LEAVING SECONDARY (GRAMMAR) SCHOOLS *AT AGE 17 YEARS OR OVER*, ENGLAND AND WALES (1910-1953)[1]

	1910-1913 (England only) %	1921 %	1926-1930 %	1935-1938 %	1948-1950 %	1951-1953 %
Free and Special Place Holders						
Boys	22·2	22·2	29·7..	29·7	33·9	34·0
Girls	43·8	46·6	38·6	29·3	32·8	33·4
Fee-Paying Pupils						
Boys	12·3	14·7	25·9	30·3 (23·5)	—	—
Girls	22·0	20·9	28·3	27·5 (22·2)	—	—

[1] *Compiled from Annual Reports of the Board (Ministry) of Education.*
NOTES: 1921. The only year in the period 1921-5 when the returns distinguish free place holders from fee-paying pupils.
Up to 1928, leavers aged 12-17 are included.
1929 and after, only leavers aged 14-17 are included.
1935-38. Part fee-payers in brackets.
1948 and after. Direct Grant grammar schools excluded.

Table 29

PROPORTION OF PUPILS LEAVING SECONDARY (GRAMMAR) SCHOOLS AT THE AGE OF 16 YEARS, ENGLAND AND WALES (1910-1953)[1]

	1910-1013 (England only) %	1921 %	1926-1930 %	1935-1938 %	1948-1950 %	1951-1953 %
Free and Special Place Holders						
Boys	21·9	29·1	39·7	42·1	41·9	49·4
Girls	24·5	20·0	34·1	44·7	41·4	47·0
Fee-Paying Pupils						
Boys	20·3	23·7	33·9	40·1 (43·6)	—	—
Girls	20·4	19·9	31·1	38·5 (40·1)	—	—

[1] *Compiled from the Annual Reports of the Board (Ministry) of Education.*

NOTES: 1921. The only year in the period 1921-25 when returns distinguished free place pupils from fee-paying pupils.
Up to 1928. Leavers aged 12-16 are included.
1929 and after, only leavers aged 14, 15 and 16 included.
1935-38. Part fee-payers in brackets.
1948 and after. Direct Grant grammar schools excluded.

Table 30

BOYS LEAVING GRAMMAR SCHOOLS, AGED UNDER 16, AND 17 AND OVER, IN SELECTED PERIODS UP TO 1939. SOUTH WEST HERTFORDSHIRE AND MIDDLESBROUGH

SOUTH WEST HERTFORDSHIRE

	1884-1900			1904-1912			YEAR OF ENTRY 1916-1918			1922-1930			1934-1938		
	N*	-16 %	17+	N	-16 %	17+	N	-16 %	17+	N	-16 %	17+	N	-16 %	17+
Free and Special Place Holders	32	81	—	114	45	30	101	25	40	191	20	37	108	19	28
Fee-Paying Pupils ..	485	81	4	314	64	11	343	65	17	411	24	36	199	24	44

MIDDLESBROUGH

	1905-1910			1911-1918			YEAR OF ENTRY 1919-1924			1925-1930			1935-1937†		
	N	-16 %	17+	N	-16 %	17+	N	-16 %	17+	N	-16 %	17+	N	-16 %	17+
Free and Special Place Holders	83	49	35	189	69	10	95	38	17	73	26	28	49	26	24
Fee-Paying Pupils ..	141	62	13	287	72	15	187	49	15	86	31	28	30	22	25

* Number of leavers, excluding pupils transferring to other schools.
† Year of leaving.

Table 31

BOYS LEAVING GRAMMAR SCHOOLS AGED UNDER 16, AND 17 AND OVER, BEFORE AND AFTER THE SECOND WORLD WAR. SOUTH WEST HERTFORDSHIRE AND MIDDLESBROUGH

	No. of Leavers*		% Leaving under 16		% Leaving 17 and over	
	1934-1938	1948-1951	1934-1938	1948-1951	1934-1938	1948-1951
SOUTH WEST HERTFORDSHIRE						
Middle-Class	53	85	6	8	62	71
Lower Middle-Class	186	156	29	10	36	56
Working-Class	57	87	18	20	25	34
All	296	328	22	12	39	54
MIDDLESBROUGH						
Middle-Class	51	52	16	8	39	44
Lower Middle-Class	93	107	17	7	27	33
Working-Class	150	201	33	15	18	20
All	294	360	24	12	25	28

* Number of Leavers, excluding pupils transferring to other schools.

Table 32

BOYS LEAVING GRAMMAR SCHOOLS WITH CERTIFICATES AND PROCEEDING TO FURTHER EDUCATION, BEFORE AND AFTER THE SECOND WORLD WAR. SOUTH WEST HERTFORDSHIRE AND MIDDLESBROUGH

	No. of Leavers*		% obtaining School Certificate		% obtaining Higher School Certificate		% Proceeding to Universities		% Proceeding to Other Institutions	
Social Class	Pre-War	Post-War	Pre-War	Post-War	Pre-War	Post-War	Pre-War	Post-War	Pre-War	Post-War
SOUTH WEST HERTFORDSHIRE (1935-38; 1948-51)										
Middle-Class ..	79	85	82	88	13	51	18	27	8	7
Lower Middle-Class	133	156	69	86	14	37	8	19	2	3
Working-Class ..	54	87	82	80	11	26	2	13	2	5
All	266	328	78	85	12	38	9	20	3	4
MIDDLESBROUGH (1935-37; 1948-50)										
Middle-Class ..	49	50	76	88	4	32	4	28	10	6
Lower Middle-Class	108	104	61	78	5	20	6	10	4	3
Working-Class ..	137	191	69	71	6	13	4	10	1	1
All	294	345	67	76	5	18	5	16	4	2

* Number of Leavers, excluding pupils transferring to other schools.

NOTE ON THE CHILDREN OF ROMAN CATHOLIC
FAMILIES IN MIDDLESBROUGH

In earlier chapters of this report, where use has been made
of school records, the Catholic grammar schools in Middlesbrough have been excluded from the analysis. Their records
are frequently of a different character from those of other
schools, making direct comparison difficult; they were until
1946, Direct Grant Schools, and have always drawn a high
proportion of their pupils from a wide area outside Middlesbrough itself. The information collected in respect of
Catholic children has therefore been analysed separately
and is presented summarily in this Note.

The Roman Catholic minority in and around Middlesbrough has grown up through immigration from Ireland and
in 1953 contributed some 20 per cent. of the child population, which was distributed among the occupational groups
as follows:

Table 33

SOCIAL ORIGINS OF CATHOLIC AND OTHER CHILDREN
ENTERING SECONDARY SCHOOLS IN MIDDLESBROUGH, 1953[1]

Father's Occupation	Catholics	Others
	%	%
Professional workers, business owners and managers	5·2	4·9
Clerical workers	0·5	5·6
Foremen, small shopkeepers, etc. ..	12·7	13·8
Skilled manual workers	36·8	40·4
Unskilled manual workers	44·8	35·3
Total	100·0	100·0
(N*)	(212)	(799)

* These figures represent a 50% sample of the age-group.

[1] From the occupational classification of parents of a 50% sample
of all children entering secondary schools in 1953.

Secondary education for these children dates from the period of expansion following the 1902 Act when two direct grant grammar schools were established, one each for boys and girls. From the beginning a minority of the places were open to competition and the proportion increased throughout the inter-war period, though not as fast as in the non-Catholic schools. However, since the middle-thirties, the Catholic grammar schools have catered for proportionately more children of humble social origin than their non-Catholic counterparts. Before 1944 the 'inferior' social composition of the Catholic population outweighed the less generous provision of free and special places in Catholic grammar schools, and working-class Catholic families also contributed a greater proportion of children to the fee-paying group than did other working-class families. Since 1944, the annual entry to the Catholic schools has been consistently more representative than the entry to other grammar schools, containing a higher proportion of boys of working-class origin and a lower proportion of lower middle-class origin. In particular, the children of unskilled workers are much better represented than in the intake to non-Catholic schools; proportionately twice as many enter annually.

Ability and Opportunity since 1945

In 1945 the Catholic Grammar schools lost their 'direct grant' status and became 'assisted' schools. Candidates for places in Catholic grammar schools are now selected by the Local Education Authority in the same way as others; any residue of places is filled by children selected by adjacent authorities.

The standard for admission to grammar schools is fixed by the Examinations Board and places are found in the Catholic grammar schools for all Catholic children reaching the required level in the selection examination. Thus, in 1933, 88 Catholic children reached the required standard (represented by a minimum IQ of about 115) and places were made available for them, accommodation being provided for an additional class of children in one of the Catholic grammar schools. However, as the following figures show, a slightly higher proportion of Catholic than of non-Catholic children of the 10-11 age-group is admitted to grammar schools.

				Catholic pupils %	Others %
1948	..	..	..	15·3	14·2
1949	..	..	..	13·1	14·9
1950	..	..	..	15·0	14·7
1951	..	..	..	15·3	14·3
1952	..	..	..	18·0	15·3
1953	..	..	..	19·3	15·0
1954	..	..	..	15·4	14·7

This is apparently the result of a different relationship between the social class, size of family, and measured intelligence of Catholic children as distinct from non-Catholic. Thus, the average level of measured intelligence of children from Catholic families at the extremes of the occupational scale was found in 1953 to be slightly higher than of children from non-Catholic families at the same social level.[1]

The children of unskilled workers form a very large group amongst the Catholics, and their relatively superior average measured intelligence must account to a great degree for the proportionately larger yield of Catholic pupils eligible for admission to grammar schools. The inverse relationship already noted for the non-Catholic population[2] between size of family and success in the selection examination did not hold in 1953 for Catholic candidates. As can be seen from the following table, although children from Catholic

	Mean IQ and Standard Deviation	
[1] Father's Occupation	Catholic pupils	Others
Professional workers, business owners and managers	121·37 (8·52)	115·24 (12·00)
Unskilled manual workers ..	98·72 (15·09)	96·50 (12·94)

[2] See p. 90 above.

families of two children were proportionately more succesful in the selection examination, there was no sharp drop in the rates of success of children from larger families comparable with that which occurred in the non-Catholic group and which reflects the well-established inverse relationship between family size and intelligence test scores.

Table 34

AWARDS OF GRAMMAR SCHOOL PLACES IN RELATION TO FAMILY SIZE. CATHOLIC AND OTHER CHILDREN

Number in family				% awarded Grammar School places Catholic pupils	Others
1	..	..	..	20·0	26·8
2	..	..	..	31·2	23·0
3	..	..	..	17·1	19·0
4 plus	..	..	..	18·2	6·0

Except in respect of the size of the family the home backgrounds of working-class children from Catholic families in our sample did not differ markedly from those of children from non-Catholic families. The children are distributed in much the same way over the different types of home distinguished for the purposes of our analysis in Chapter 6. Thus:

Table 35

HOME ENVIRONMENT OF CATHOLIC AND OTHER WORKING-CLASS CHILDREN

Type of Home	Catholic pupils %	Others %
1. Wholly favourable	12·0	13·2
2. One aspect favourable only		
(a) Environment ..	8·1	9·0
(b) Parents' attitude ..	31·0	33·2
3. Wholly unfavourable ..	48·9	44·6
Total	100·0	100·0
(N)*	(184)	(590)

* These figures represent a 50% sample of the age-group of working-class children in Roman Catholic primary schools.

However, as can be seen from Table 36 below, a higher
proportion of Catholic than of non-Catholic working-class
children obtained entry to grammar schools in 1953 from
each of the types of home classified as favourable or unfavourable in all or any of the features taken into account:

Table 36

AWARDS OF GRAMMAR SCHOOL PLACES IN RELATION TO HOME
BACKGROUND. CATHOLIC AND OTHER WORKING-CLASS
CHILDREN

| Type of Home | % gaining grammar school places | |
	Catholic pupils	Others
1. Wholly favourable	31·8 (22)	21·8 (78)
2. One aspect favourable only		
(a) Environment	33·3 (15)	11·3 (53)
(b) Parents' attitudes ..	21·1 (57)	13·8 (196)
3. Wholly unfavourable ..	7·8 (90)	4·6 (263)
Total (N)*	16·8 (184)	10·5 (590)

* The figures represent a 50% sample of the age-group of working-
class children in Roman Catholic primary schools.

CONCLUSIONS

O UR enquiries took as their starting point the account of the history of the social distribution of educational opportunity which emerged from the investigation into occupational selection and mobility undertaken at the London School of Economics in 1949. The object was to look more closely than was possible on a national scale into the part played by the educational system in the process of social selection, and at the impact of the Education Act of 1944 on the particular role of the grammar schools. This is an account of the first stage of the work which is being undertaken in a traditionally prosperous district in the south of England—the South West Educational Division of Hertfordshire—and in an industrial county borough in the north —Middlesbrough, Yorkshire—which has had a chequered economic history and in which educational reform has had to face greater material difficulties.

In the years of our enquiry in both areas, virtually the full quota of boys with the necessary minimum IQ from each occupational group in the population were awarded places in grammar schools. If by 'ability' we mean 'measured intelligence' and by 'opportunity' access to grammar schools, then opportunity may be said to stand in close relationship with ability in both these areas today. Though they are not in any strict sense representative areas they are by no means untypical of their kind, and we may reasonably conclude that in very many, if not in most, parts of the country the chances of children at a given level of ability entering grammar schools are no longer dependent on their social origins.

The story of educational change leading up to this achievement in South West Hertfordshire and Middlesbrough illustrates the way in which the social and educa-

tional pressures of the national situation worked themselves
out under very different local conditions.

In the nineteenth century educational provision was
frankly viewed in terms of occupation and class. Secondary
education led to middle-class occupations; elementary
instruction was for workmen and servants. If a conspicu-
ously able child of the working-class received the education
appropriate to middle-class children, he owed it to success in
the competition for scarce scholarships provided by private
charity. In South West Hertfordshire and Middlesbrough,
as elsewhere, scholarships were provided 'to enable boys and
girls of exceptional ability to proceed from the Elementary
schools to the Endowed schools', and in the early days of the
educational ladder the middle-class prerogative was
anxiously watched. In 1904, the headmaster of the Watford
Grammar School saw 'no element of difficulty or danger' in
having 10 per cent. of his scholars drawn from the elementary schools; in his opinion it constituted sufficient provision
'for enabling poor boys of exceptional ability to rise from
the elementary to the secondary schools'.

In the generation which followed the 1902 Act there was
an unprecedented expansion of secondary education in
which the grammar schools in South West Hertfordshire and
Middlesbrough played their part. In 1892 there were well-
informed complaints of public apathy towards 'intermediate' education,[1] but thirty years later, the situation had
been transformed. Every year after the First World War a
greater number of parents sent their children to the secondary schools as fee-payers. Competition for the safety and
prestige of a black-coated job was growing keener and a
secondary education became an indispensable investment
to secure a good occupational prospect. The provision of
free secondary education was related to the demand for
fee-paying places when in 1907 official policy stipulated that

---

[1] A. H. D. Acland and H. Llewellyn Smith (eds.), *Studies in Secondary Education.* 1892, p. xxvii.

a number of free places should be provided annually in schools on the Grant List proportionate to the total number of pupils admitted in the previous year.

Even before the First World War more than one-quarter of the growing total number of places in the grammar schools in both areas were open to competition. As the proportion grew, after the war, the middle-class and lower middle-class character of the schools was undermined, slowly in South West Hertfordshire and quite rapidly in Middlesbrough, by the inflow of pupils of working-class origin. To some observers equality of opportunity already appeared to be a reality in the 1920's. Lord Birkenhead went so far as to claim that 'the number of scholarships from the elementary schools (is) not limited, awards being made to all children who show capacity to profit'.[1]

The assumption that the educational ladder was for the exclusive use of the gifted poor became more and more unreal with each increase in the provision of places open to competition, and the expansion of the grammar schools had profound effects upon the social composition of the primary, then called 'elementary', schools. These schools, and through them the competition for free places in grammar schools, were always open to those of the middle- and lower middle-classes who cared to use them. The small minority of parents who could afford to realize higher aspirations for their children sent them to independent schools, and others used the private schools and the preparatory departments of the grammar schools. But an increasing number sent their children, especially their sons, through the rough and tumble of the elementary schools.

The result was that as the scholarship ladder widened it carried an increasing number of middle-class boys, and the competitive strength of working-class boys declined. After 1933, when economies were introduced to meet the economic depression, a place won in competition meant,

[1] Quoted in K. Lindsay, op. cit., p. 9.

more often than not, partial rather than total remission of fees, and the selection examination was opened to children attending private schools as well as public elementary schools. Boys of middle-class origin, and particularly those from lower middle-class families of clerks, small business people, tradesmen, etc., took up an increasing share of fee-paying places; they also improved their competitive strength with every increase in the number of places open to award. The long-term decline in the competitive strength of working-class boys was as marked in South West Hertfordshire, where the proportion of places open to award remained virtually constant up to the Second World War, as in Middlesbrough, where, by 1937, 80 per cent. were open to award. The abolition of fees in 1945 accentuated the decline in both areas.[1]

The effect of these developments on the social composition of the schools themselves naturally depended upon the proportion of places open to competition. In South West Hertfordshire the grammar school was the undisputed preserve of middle-class, and especially of lower middle-class boys who, by 1939, represented two-thirds of the annual intake. When all places were opened to competition in 1945, these boys suffered severe competition and today constitute only one-third of the entry. In Middlesbrough working-class boys formed 40 per cent. or more of the annual intake throughout the decade after 1935, and the abolition of fees has not brought about any drastic change in the social composition of the schools such as has taken place in South West Hertfordshire.[2]

It is obvious that the number of working-class boys entering the grammar schools each year has been increasing fast, and that there are more in the schools today than ever before. Nevertheless, the probability that a working-class boy will get to a grammar school is not strikingly different

---

[1] p. 37 above.
[2] pp. 26-28 above.

from what it was before 1945, and there are still marked differences in the chances which boys of different social origins have of obtaining a place. Of those working-class boys who reached the age of 11 in the years 1931-41 rather less than 10 per cent. entered selective secondary schools.[1] In 1953 the proportion of working-class boys admitted to grammar schools was 12 per cent. in Middlesbrough and 14 per cent. in South West Hertfordshire. Thus, approximately one working-class boy in eight was admitted in Middlesbrough, as compared, for instance, with nearly one in three of the sons of clerks; and approximately one working-class boy in seven in South West Hertfordshire, as compared with nearly one in two of the sons of clerks.

Our findings as to the social distribution of measured intelligence are closely consistent with those of earlier enquiries, and provide an adequate explanation of these differences. Virtually the full quota of boys with the requisite minimum IQ from every class was admitted to grammar schools and the distribution of opportunity stands today in closer relationship to that of ability (as measured by intelligence tests) than ever before.[2] Yet the problem of inequality of educational opportunity is not thereby disposed of.

We have considered some of the material and cultural differences in the environment of the children who succeed, as distinct from those who do not succeed, in the selection examination for secondary education, and we have shown how the success of children varies with the distribution of these features of the environment even at the same social level. Since measured intelligence is so closely related to the results of the selection procedure our findings are relevant to the problem of the influence of environment on intelligence test scores. But this was not our direct concern, and the features of the environment we have selected for study

---

[1] cf. Glass, D. V. (ed.), op. cit., p. 129.
[2] Table 8, p. 61 above.

cannot, of course, be regarded as social determinants of intelligence. Nevertheless, though they touch on less fundamental problems, certain conclusions do emerge concerning the part played by differences of environment in the social distribution of educational opportunity.

In the past, the problem of social waste in education could be seen in comparatively simple terms, for gross material factors overshadowed all others. Poverty caused ill-health and poor attendance; facilities for study could not be provided in slum homes, nor proper instruction given in overcrowded schools; grammar school places were refused by parents who could not afford to forgo adolescent earnings. But the influence on the distribution of educational opportunity of the material environment in which children live at home and are taught at school before the age of selection, is tending to diminish in importance in face of the general prosperity and the measures of social reform which are characteristic of post-war Britain. Social factors influencing educational selection reveal themselves in more subtle forms today.

The present situation at its most favourable is illustrated by the position in South West Hertfordshire where a generally high minimum degree of material comfort is enjoyed at all social levels. In that area, in 1952, material conditions in their homes did not, at a given social level, distinguish the successful from the unsuccessful candidate in the selection examination. At a given social level, the children who secured grammar school places were not those whose parents earned the highest income, nor those who enjoyed superior standards of housing.[1] On the other hand, differences in the size of the family, and in the education, attitudes and ambitions of parents were reflected in the examination performance of children in all classes.[2] In Middlesbrough the situation was less favourable. In 1953 in

---

[1] p. 89 above.
[2] pp. 88 and 90 above.

that area, purely material conditions at home still differentiated the successful from the unsuccessful children even at the same social level.[1] If poor parents were favourably disposed towards their children's education this attitude was less likely than in South West Hertfordshire to be reflected in the performance of their children in the selection examination.[2] Moreover, the traditional association between poor homes and poor schools persists in Middlesbrough,[3] and places an additional handicap on the child of poor but educationally well-disposed parents. There is still scope for attack on gross economic disabilities. In South West Hertfordshire, however, virtually everyone enjoys an adequate basic income and good housing which, together with the security of the social services, provide something like the basic ingredients of a middle-class or at least lower middle-class existence. The influence of the home on children's educational prospects is more subtle, and the problem of developing and utilizing their ability to the full is educational rather than social.

Once the grosser material handicaps are eliminated, the size of the family emerges as the most important single index of the favourable or unfavourable influence of home environment on educational prospects. Very little is known as to what determines the size of families at different social levels, but there is no doubt about the existence of a relationship between family size and educational opportunity. This relationship obviously has its economic aspect, even in the Welfare State. It is a well-established fact, however, that children from small families, at all social levels, tend on the average to do better in intelligence tests and therefore also in the selection examination for secondary education. Dr. Nisbet has suggested[4] that the child of a large family learns verbal skills less effectively from his peers than

---

[1] p. 89 above.
[2] p. 89 above.
[3] p. 74 above.
[4] op. cit.

does the child of a small family from adults, and that he carries the handicap at least until the age of eleven. But the evidence from Middlesbrough suggests that the educational disadvantages of a large family are far less marked for the children of Catholic parents,[1] and if generally true this would cast doubt on the notion that there is some distinctive quality of educational value in the environment of a small family. It may be suggested that family limitation amongst Catholic parents does not correspond so closely to intelligence as it tends to do amongst non-Catholic parents, so that the average level of ability of children from large Catholic families is likely to be higher than of those from large non-Catholic families. In fact, the mean IQ of the children of Catholic unskilled workers, who constituted the largest single social group amongst the Catholic children, was found in 1953 to be slightly higher than that of others at this social level.[2] This finding cannot be interpreted without more information, particularly as to the geographical origins of Catholic parents, and their length of residence in Middlesbrough. Recent immigrants to the area might be temporarily employed in occupations below their capacities, so that their offspring might show greater ability than the average for the unskilled group. However that may be, this problem, and others in the same field of the relations between social class, family environment and educational opportunity, can only be effectively examined through intensive enquiry into children's home environment on case-study lines.

The social waste at the point of selection indicted by Kenneth Lindsay in the 1920's has today been pushed forward *into* the grammar schools where it now occurs at the threshold of the Sixth Form. In both areas, as nationally, there are marked differences, according to their social origins, in the length of school life and opportunity for

---

[1] cf. p. 137 above.
[2] p. 136 (footnote) above.

further education enjoyed by children at the same general level of ability.[1] It is possible that material differences in home background come into their own again here, even in South West Hertfordshire, underlying and reinforcing differences of attitude to the value of an extended secondary course and further education on the part of parents and children alike.

However, it seems doubtful, on the evidence available to us, whether parents can be held wholly responsible, at least so far as their early intentions are concerned, for the wastage of children from secondary schools before or when they reach the age of 16. It is evident that their strength of purpose as well as their capacity to make sacrifices on behalf of their children's education varies from class to class. But there has undoubtedly been a post-war revolution in parents' attitudes towards their children's education, especially at the bottom of the social scale. The frustration of parents whose children are sent to other secondary schools despite their wish that they should attend grammar schools is not confined to the middle-classes. The frustrated minorities of skilled and unskilled working-class parents in Middlesbrough and South West Hertfordshire were proportionately not so very much smaller than in the lower middle-class, and in absolute numbers they were, of course, much larger.[2] Moreover, working-class parents who said that they wished their children to attend a grammar school also said, in the great majority of cases, that they were willing to keep them at school at least until the age of 16; and a surprisingly large proportion contemplated a leaving age of 18 or over (one-quarter in Middlesbrough and nearly one-third in South West Hertfordshire).[3] Admittedly, the proportion of middle-class and lower middle-class parents contemplating a six or seven year secondary course for their children was larger and it is often argued that it would be expedient to take this

---

[1] p. 118 ff. above.
[2] p. 78 above.
[3] p. 79 above.

into account in making the selection, at least at the border-line of differences in ability. But it would be difficult on ethical and political grounds to justify such an evasion of a problem which should be regarded as an educational challenge to the schools. Each generation of more or less able children allowed to leave school before or immediately after completing the minimum course (or denied admittance because of their suspected intention of doing so) ensures a recurrence of the wastage in the next generation, even allow-ing for the possibility that in a number of cases parents may regret their own lack of educational qualifications and encourage their children to take opportunities which they themselves missed.

It is tempting to regard the problem as merely one of 'assimilation' into selective secondary schools with a dis-tinctive tradition and rather specific educational aspirations. The secondary grammar schools, despite considerable regional variety in their social composition, are by tradition schools serving the middle-classes. Their traditions and ethos tend to be foreign to the boy or girl of working-class origins and the problem of assimilation is a real one. A small and highly selected minority of working-class free-place pupils may be expected to be assimilated—to become in effect socially mobile, accepting school values, making the most of the course by remaining at school at least until the age of 16 or, in some cases, until a later age and going on to full-time further education. But when, as is now the case, the grammar school is open to a much wider population, assimilation is more difficult and this approach to the problem becomes less and less fruitful.

The precise nature of the hindrances placed by their home background in the way of educating working-class children in grammar schools urgently needs investigating both for its own sake as an immediate problem of educational organization, and for the light it would throw on the problems and possibilities of the comprehensive school. But in the long run, the problem must be viewed as part of the broader question of the interaction of homes and schools generally—of the influence of the home at each social level on the educability of children in schools of particular types and with particular traditions and aims. The problem of equality of educational opportunity is now more complicated than when it took the simple form of the need to secure free access to grammar schools on equal intellectual terms. With the expansion of educational opportunity and the reduction of gross economic handicaps to children's school performance the need arises to understand the optimum conditions for the integration of school and home environment at all social levels in such a way as to minimize the educational disadvantages of both and to turn their educational advantages to full account.

NOTE ON THE CLASSIFICATION OF OCCUPATIONS

The categories of the 'B' Code used by the Government Social Survey are defined as follows:

(a) *Professional and Higher Technical Grades*

All persons included in this class are those whose occupations require special training. Thus doctors, State Registered nurses, ordained ministers, teachers, surveyors, engineers, etc., are included. But welfare workers, actors, and others in similar occupations are not included.

(b) *Business Owners and Managers*

This category includes higher executives and administrators in industry and commerce, who are not also specialists, Members of Parliament, owners of large businesses, and officers above the rank of Warrant Officer in H.M. Forces. It differs from category (d) below in that, whilst inspectional and supervisory workers are in charge of others, they do not control policy matters.

(c) *Clerical Grades*

Junior bank clerks, articled clerks, cashiers, book-keepers, 'progress chasers', junior draughtsmen and desk workers generally.

(d) *Foremen, Small Shopkeepers, etc.*

Charge hands and foremen of small gangs, viewers, over-lookers and managers of small shops; persons who are in charge of others, but who are not qualified to be classed as managerial or professional workers; men and women with small authority, excluding those in the clerical grades.

(e) *Miscellaneous Other Grades*

Non-ordained ministers and religious workers, social workers, club leaders, insurance agents, actors, professional sportsmen, police, etc.

(*f*) *Skilled Manual Workers*

All persons engaged upon manual work which requires a special training and/or acquired skill and/or responsibility for a process or operation. Improvers and apprentices, but not labourers, are included.

(*g*) *Unskilled Manual Workers*

All persons, other than clerical workers, who are engaged in any occupation which could be performed without (i) Vocational training; (ii) Application of acquired skills; (iii) An education beyond the primary stage; (iv) Much other training or any considerable degree of knowledge.

This category includes cleaners, messengers, lift attendants, navvies, counter hands, machine minders on simple processes, craftsmen's 'mates', cement mixers, etc.

NOTE ON THE STATISTICAL RELIABILITY
OF TABLES

The numbers in our samples of children leaving primary schools in South West Hertfordshire in 1952 and Middlesbrough in 1953, and secondary schools in various other years in these areas, are too small when broken down for purpose of analysis in terms of social class, home or school background, to yield differences which we can be certain are due to causes other than chance (i.e. which can be shown to be statistically significant). It does not, of course, follow that differences which cannot be shown to be statistically significant are illusory or necessarily due to chance. Readers are nevertheless warned that the percentages which relate to the samples of the 10-11 age group of children in the single years of our enquiry, or to school leavers in the years for which information was collected from school records, are subject to considerable error from chance fluctuations, so that the conclusions based on them must be regarded as, to that extent, tentative.

INDEX OF AUTHORS

Acland, A. H. D., 140(n)

Bell, Hugh, 9
Birkenhead, Lord, 141
Board of Education, xv, 10, 12, 13, 14, 20, 35, 113, 115, 128-130;
    letter to Governors, 12(n), 13
Central Advisory Council for Education, 113-4, 115, 117, 124, 124(n)
Chisholm, Cecil, 4(n)
Corlett, T., 71

Dale, R., 124
Davies, H., 27

Floud, J. E., xviii(n), 21

Glass, D. V., xiii(n), xv, xviii(n), 21, 33, 143
Glass, Ruth, xiv, xvii, 24, 70, 95, 99
Government Social Survey, 18, 151-2
Gray, J. L., xvii, xvii(n), 48, 51, 52(n)
Gray, P. G., 71

Halsey, A. H., 18, 96, 113, 118
Hans, N., xvii
Hogben, Professor, xvii, xvii(n), 51

Leybourne-White, G., xvii(n)
Lindsay, K., xvi(n), 95, 141, 146
Llewellyn-Smith, H., 140(n)

Moshinsky, Miss P., xvii, xvii(n), 48, 51, 52(n)

Nisbet, J. D., 91, 137, 145

Registrar-General, 4, 6, 7, 17

Vernon, P. E., 65

Wartime Social Survey, 5(n)